D0374557

"Peter Smith is first and foremost an educator who understands that life itself can be the key to learning. Peter and I served in Congress together, and he became the President of CSU Monterey Bay, a campus I helped establish on a former military base at Fort Ord. Peter understands change and that in a changing world, education cannot be limited by the restrictions and barriers of the past. It must be about results—the development of the human potential in all of us. This book is an important guide to a new approach to learning. When life itself in changing dramatically, so must we and so must the learning process."

LEON E. PANETTA
Former U.S. Secretary of Defense

"This book is badly needed by millions of people, and I would bet you know some of them. They are the people who didn't go to college the first time around and want another chance.

Luckily, there are a lot of ways to get that other chance and Peter Smith's excellent book describes many alternatives. You can acquire credentials—and degrees—in ways that fit your life better than a program at a traditional college.

I warmly recommend this book to adult learners and to those (like their parents and employers) who are trying to help them."

DONALD E. GRAHAM
Chairman, Graham Holdings Co.
Former Owner of the *Washington Post*

"The future of education is one where it never ends, and Peter Smith provides an essential guide to this new learning economy. Full of compelling stories and engaging interviews, *Free-Range Learning in the Digital Age* is a roadmap for learners of all ages and backgrounds."

JEFFREY J. SELINGO
New York Times best-selling author of
There Is Life After College and *College (Un)bound*

"*Free-Range Learning in the Digital Age* hits directly upon the typical journey of the adult learner; one who has some formal learning and many informal learning experiences, or, as Peter Smith puts it, "hidden credentials." This book is timely in that it addresses workforce learning and futuristic learning environments for children and adults alike. It is a go-to guide for learners, teachers, and administrators."

DR. JILL BUBAN, SR.
Director of Research & Innovation, Online Learning Consortium

"WOW; an enjoyable read about innovative pedagogy. That alone would be a good enough reason to read this book by Peter Smith. An even better reason, however, is that this book is terrifically informative and insightful about how "free-range learning" in today's context provides myriad ways in which adults beyond the traditional age of college can successfully pursue serious higher learning. This is true whether this pursuit is to gain the knowledge a person wants and needs in seeking specific job skills, simply expanding her or his knowledge base for the pure enjoyment of doing so, or perhaps most importantly to receive legitimate credit for the learning she or he has already experienced, whether in a college setting or not. The comfortable blending of specific descriptions of various forms of adult learning opportunities and personal examples of individuals from various walks of life make this book a valuable resource for adults contemplating engaging in a new form of learning.

This book is written for a lay audience, not for the professional higher-education crowd. Yet it does a great job of including evidence of success or lack thereof, not just hype, about the various innovations in "free-range learning" currently available. Not every good idea is captured in the book, yet it certainly provides a wide range of types of experience that a person might want to pursue. And Peter Smith's own lifelong experience with adult and experiential learning, both as a policy maker and practitioner in the public and private sectors of American and international higher education, provides a depth of knowledge and experience on which a lay audience can rely. I highly recommend this book for any adult considering returning to the world of higher education, whether to receive further credentialing or not. You'll learn a lot that will be helpful to you in making a decision about what novel new approach might work best for you, and I'll bet you'll enjoy the read as well."

DAVID LONGENECKER
Former CEO of the Western Interstate Commission of Higher Education

"Peter Smith has hit the nail on the head! Through a very personal lens, this longtime education leader and disruptor writes a very smart and timely book that depicts that all people are inherently lifetime learners. The time is now via technology and alternative learning and assessment providers to fight the "knowledge discrimination" whereby traditional higher-ed institutions and employers fail to recognize very important diverse sources of lifelong learning. Peter demands that we take charge of our learning and career destinies."

DEBORAH QUAZZO
Cofounder ASU GSV Summit, Managing Partner GSV Acceleration Fund

"There has been a lot written about the changing ways that people are gaining access to post-secondary education. Most of it is abstract and speculative based on the growing use and availability of digital resources. Peter Smith brings all this to a personal level. The readers of *Free-Range Learning in the Digital Age* will be able to understand how real people at different points in their lives need and can use these expanding digital opportunities." Readers will learn how educational innovators are opening new pathways for different types of learners. They are also guided through ways they can assess what type of pathway will suit their own unique circumstances. Peter Smith has really made this emerging field understandable to anyone curious about enriching their lives and careers through accessible further education.

SALLY JOHNSTONE
CEO, National Center of Higher-Education Management Systems

"Early in *Free-Range Learning* Peter Smith invokes the *The Wizard of Oz*, where the Scarecrow, the leader of Dorothy's little band, bemoans his lack of a brain. The Wizard sets him straight: the brain has been there all along; what was lacking was a *diploma*. The Wizard, and Dr. Smith, both recognize that what we know, what we have learned through work, school, social interactions, and everything else that humans do has real value. As a serial college president, congressman, and policy maker, Smith also knows that a piece of paper does not create knowledge, but he explains why validating knowledge that has been gained is so important for adults and why adult learning, to be successful, must allow for multiple pathways that fit every individual. Through interviews with learners and a new generation of educators who see learning as an eternally continuing process, interspersed with descriptions of emerging technologies and approaches, Smith describes a promising future for securing a truly educated and informed citizenry. The title is perhaps something of a misnomer: Smith has set out guideposts that both learners and educators would do well to follow."

MICHAEL GOLDSTEIN
Partner Cooley Associates

FREE-RANGE LEARNING IN THE DIGITAL AGE

To Caroline —

a colleague in arms!

Peter Smith

5/23/18

FREE-RANGE LEARNING IN THE DIGITAL AGE

The Emerging Revolution in College, Career, and Education

PETER P. SMITH

SelectBooks

NEW YORK

Copyright © 2018 by Peter Plympton Smith

This edition published by SelectBooks, Inc.

For information address SelectBooks, Inc., New York, New York.

First Edition

ISBN 978-1-59079-452-4

Library of Congress Cataloging-in-Publication Data

Names: Smith, Peter, 1945- author.
Title: Free-Range Learning : The Emerging Revolution in College, Career, and
Education / Peter P. Smith.
Description: New York : SelectBooks, [2018] | Includes bibliographical
references and index.
Identifiers: LCCN 2017057104 | ISBN 9781590794524 (pbk. trade book : alk.
paper)
Subjects: LCSH: Professional education–United States. | Continuing
education–United States. | Adult college students–United States.
Classification: LCC LC1072.C56 S65 2018 | DDC 378/.013–dc23 LC record
available at https://lccn.loc.gov/2017057104

Manufactured in the United States of America

10 9 8 7 6 5 4 3 2 1

CONTENTS

FOREWORD

THIS BOOK IS A MUST-READ for anyone who has gained a host of skills and experience in life but whose career has smacked head-on with what we might call the parchment ceiling—the lack of a college degree. Most "career books" tell you how to make the most of your degree. This one tells you how you can make the most of earning a degree and also how to pursue an altogether different kind of rewarding path without a degree.

The book's author possesses a remarkable perspective from which to offer ingenious suggestions. He actually started a university—a very successful one. He has earned his doctorate degree and has served in the United States Congress. And he is currently a professor at one of the nation's most creative and effective schools when it comes to serving the unique educational needs of adults.

In the following pages you will meet people who have overcome or circumvented the lack of formal "certificates of knowledge." As this is written, there are over six million unfilled jobs in the United States, and many are high paying and personally rewarding. The problem is that the candidates for these jobs do not possess the educational or training certification employers demand for these jobs. Ironically, even at the height of the recent Great Recession there were three million such jobs—once again unfilled because of real or perceived mismatches between job descriptions and qualifications of job seekers.

Too often "uncredentialed knowledge" becomes unrecognized knowledge. This is a disservice to employees and potential employers alike. As a former employer myself who once led a corporation with 180,000 employees, half of whom had college degrees, I do feel compelled to offer a bit of defense of the "credential system"—while at the same time recognizing its shortcomings and especially its unfairness. Employers need to have some means of knowing whether the people they hire possess the knowledge and skills needed to fill the jobs they will take; thus the dependence upon degrees and certifications. Fortunately, as described in this book, there are a growing number of ways to overcome the obstacles that have resulted. The author describes this process as making the most of "free-range" learning.

The fundamental point is that a classroom is not the only place in life where a person learns. One's brain is not programmed to automatically shut down as soon as we leave a formal academic environment. One of my favorite stories demonstrating this is an incident that took place when our company had received a significant contract to remove 8,000 pounds of weight from the giant external fuel tank that we were building for NASA. The tank served as the backbone of the Space Shuttle stack. I once calculated that the fuel tank was so large that if it were placed on its side, the Wright Brothers' famous flight could have taken place entirely inside it! At that time we had built about ten of these fuel tanks and had delivered them to Cape Kennedy, gleaming in their coats of white paint.

But after eliminating about 7,200 pounds of weight, the engineers seemed to hit a wall. One day, a group of engineers were standing around a work table debating what they should do when a fellow who worked in the factory happened to pass by and overheard their conversation. After listening intently for a time, he suggested, "Why don't you *not* paint the fuel tank white?"

One of the engineers is said to have answered, "Because space hardware is always painted white." After a bit more reflection about the feebleness of that answer, a rush to the computers began, and it was determined that the paint weighed . . . yes, 800 pounds. That is why after the first few launches of the Space Shuttle the color of its fuel tank was no longer white. It was the natural orange color of the spray-on foam insulation that covered the tank!

Indeed, there are many people who could make important contributions in life and business if only they were given the opportunity. One of my grandfathers was such a man. In his autobiography he wrote "I got some schooling whenever there was some free time." He only made it through fourth grade, but as an adult he quoted Shakespeare and Milton and, among other things, constructed a machine that demonstrated how the planets move around the sun. My father completed eighth grade before he had to go to work to help support the family, yet he helped me with my math most of my way through high school.

Yes, there are many people who could make important contributions—and probably enjoy more satisfying lives in the process—if only they had the opportunity. Thanks to the sacrifices of my parents and the support of many others, including people I never met who provided scholarships, I was one of the lucky ones.

Today, as Dr. Smith describes in this book, there are increasing opportunities for a person without a college degree to earn one. The rewards are immense. The go far beyond an ability to penetrate the parchment ceiling of the career world to enjoy the financial benefits. History shows that the rewards include living a longer, healthier life, having greater self-confidence and enjoying a more stable marriage.

For example, in monetary terms alone, the median earnings of a college graduate between the ages of 25 and 34 are 70 percent greater than what a high school graduate earns, and the median earnings of the holder of an associate's degree are 20 percent higher than those of a high school graduate. During the Great Recession, individuals with a baccalaureate degree experienced about a five percent unemployment rate, while individuals with an associate's degree had ten percent unemployment, and those with a high school diploma or less suffered from joblessness at a rate of fifteen percent.

But a college degree is not for everyone. Some simply cannot afford it, some cannot fit it into their other life responsibilities, and some simply are not interested in pursuing further formal education. Fortunately, highly satisfying alternative paths can be pursued, as described in these pages.

While 86 percent of college graduates say college was a good investment—and this number will hopefully increase—college *is* expensive. The average "sticker price" of a year at a public university in America is now $9,700 and at a private institution is $33,500. That adds up to about $40,000 to $135,000 for an individual who obtains a degree within four years—which a lot of people don't. Further, as many states disinvest in higher education, the financial burden of earning a degree has increasingly shifted toward the student in the form of charging them higher tuition and fees. Adding to this conundrum is that a high school diploma by itself is worth less and less in today's competitive job market. In 1940, fewer than five percent of Americans age 25 possessed a bachelor's degree; today, the number having these degrees at this age is one-third—with 60 percent having at least some college.

But how do you demonstrate your hidden credentials, as the author calls them, if you must have a specific certified credential before you can demonstrate your *real* credentials? It's a "catch-22." I once encountered such a circumstance myself, but in a rather curious way. Trained as an aerospace engineer with a master's degree and a sizeable collection of undergraduate and graduate math courses, I had hoped, especially given the appalling lack of qualified math teachers in America's secondary schools, that one day I could teach algebra in a middle school. I had even prepared myself for a teaching career by tutoring advanced calculus during college—for 50 cents an hour! Years later, after taking early retirement from my job as a CEO, I was finally ready to set out on my new career.

But there was a catch here, too! I learned I was deemed "unqualified" to teach math in *any* public school in my state—or, as I later learned, in most states. Why? Because I didn't possess a teaching certificate (and couldn't join the union). Unlike many similar stories, mine had a happy ending: The dean of engineering at Princeton heard that I wanted to teach and asked if I would join the faculty of the School of Engineering and Applied Science at Princeton—and I gladly did.

Whatever the circumstances are, the importance of having degrees and credentials is likely to accelerate in the current globalized job market. Dame Frances Cairncross, noted journalist and academic, was a Senior Editor at *The Economist* when she wrote a book titled *The Death of Distance.* Indeed it is dead. Today, people fly around the world at nearly the speed of sound, and information flies around the world truly at the speed of light.

I have a young friend who likes to play chess. He lives in New York City, and his chess teacher lives in Los Angeles. They play via the web. Then there is the fellow in Paris who had his gall bladder removed by a surgeon in New York using a remotely controlled robot.

As the fields of artificial intelligence and robotics race forward, many more jobs at the lower end of the employment spectrum will undoubtedly be destroyed. Consider the impact of self-driving vehicles that now seem to be coming down the road faster than many had imagined. What, for example, is to become of the 3.5 million truck drivers who currently ride America's highways?

Hopefully, as in the past, more routine jobs can be replaced by more personally rewarding and higher-paying jobs. But performing those new jobs will require greater education and skill sets.

Fortunately, just as the world of employment is changing, so are the pathways to obtain degrees, apprenticeships, and certificates of attainment. And not a moment too soon, given that arguably no institutions have more successfully resisted change over the past 300 years than those of higher education. But today a student need not appear at a prescribed time to join 200 other students to listen to a sage on the stage. Instead, they have the alternative of attending lectures and studies whenever and wherever it suits their own schedules. They can carry the world's largest library around with them in their pocket. Personalized digital tutors can teach individuals much the same way a private tutor adapts pedagogy to fit an individual learner. Furthermore, education and training are becoming more adult friendly as they increasingly embrace experiential learning—partly by building ties to those who will one day hire their products.

For those not seeking an academic degree, there are growing opportunities to obtain certificates in fields that range from health care to digital technology and from carpentry to robot repair. As Yogi Berra famously advised: "When you come to a fork in the road, take it!"

But overcoming the parchment barrier, as important—and feasible—as it is, will not be the end of the journey. Knowledge is expanding so rapidly, particularly technological knowledge, that absent lifetime learning one can unwittingly become obsolescent within a few years after receiving a college degree or certificate in a specific work skill. Craig Barrett, the former CEO of Intel, has said that 90 percent of the revenues that firm records on the last day of any given year come from products that didn't even exist on the first day of that year! The half-life of knowledge is becoming ever shorter. Fortunately, this can be accommodated through combinations of continuing experiential learning and traditional classroom learning.

The alternative is, as the Red Queen advises Alice in Lewis Carroll's *Through the Looking Glass*, "Here, you see, it takes all the running you can do, to keep in the same place. If you want to get somewhere else, you must run at least twice as fast as that!" I must confess that, only partially in humor, I once proposed that college diplomas should have expiration dates printed on them!

The first step in breaking the parchment ceiling is probably the hardest: making the decision to do so. But you are not alone—help is on the way. It's never too late. I have a friend who each semester takes a course at the University of Maryland. He is 83 years old, and I don't believe he is preparing for a new career. There's just a great deal of self-satisfaction in learning. Simply focus on something that you enjoy—that is where you will be most likely to succeed.

As the adage says, "When opportunity knocks, try to answer the door." This book describes many such doors.

NORMAN AUGUSTINE
Retired Chairman and CEO, Lockheed Martin
Former Under Secretary, U.S. Army

ACKNOWLEDGMENTS

NO ONE WRITES A BOOK of any kind without great support from those around him. I want to give great thanks to my colleagues at the University of Maryland University College in general, and President Javier Miyares, more specifically, for their encouragement and support throughout the process.

Also, the people who worked with me to get the interviews that are the core of the book were instrumental in helping me get the information around which the book is built. They include Anant Agarwal, Burck Smith, Jamai Blivin, Steve Yadzinski, Jonathan Finklestein, Brenda Perea, Devon Ritter, Barbara Lomonaco, Lisa Lutz, Brandon Busteed, Matt Sigelman, Chuck Brodsky, Rob Smariga, Michael Roark, Mark Milliron, and Troy Markowitz. And thanks to my other presidential colleagues—Joyce Judy, Ed Klonoski, Tom Greene, Chris Bustamente, Paul LeBlanc—for their help.

Closer to home, my wife, Letitia Chambers, an amazing professional, has been a constant source of love, encouragement, and support throughout the process of creating the book. And thanks to Sally Johnstone and David Longanecker for their willingness to read and comment on early drafts and offer critique.

Finally, as I have written and edited my books, I have come to understand just how much I have learned from my colleagues and the learners in all of the venues where I have had the privilege of working and serving since 1970. They have been the source of my continuing professional education and development. I dedicate this book to Letitia, my colleagues mentioned above, and all of these lifelong colleagues and friends.

Free-Range Learning is the latest of several books that I have written over the last thirty years, including *Your Hidden Credentials: The Value of Learning Outside of College, The Quiet Crisis: How Higher Education Is Failing America*, and *Harnessing America's Wasted Talent: A New Ecology of Learning.*

They each pertain, one way or the other, to experiential learning and the reform of postsecondary education. Taken collectively, they represent my evolving understanding of these issues and their importance. I have drawn on material and ideas from these earlier books in writing *Free-Range Learning* where I thought doing so would be pertinent and helpful. After all, why not use parts of an interview, an idea, or a metaphor that has become even more pertinent over the years. So when you read terms such as "hidden credentials," "turning points," "transitions," and "adult-friendly colleges," they are terms that I have used throughout my professional and writing career.

I hope you enjoy the read!

INTRODUCTION

FREE-RANGE LEARNING IN THE DIGITAL AGE describes the silent learning revolution occurring in America. Many are not aware of this explosion of a vast scope and range of educational resources now available to adult learners.

If you are one of the millions of Americans who has a high school diploma and no college degree, this book is for you. If you are trapped in a job that you don't like and you know is beneath your capabilities, this book is for you. If you have a degree, but are stuck when it comes to improving your personal situation or getting the job that you want, this book is for you. If you just want to "learn your own way," not the way a parent, a college, or an employer tells you to learn, this book is also for you. Or if you are an educator, policymaker, employer, or a person who advises others on learning opportunities, this book is for you, as well.

The plain fact is that millions of Americans have historically faced huge barriers to getting the education and the jobs that they want. Since the end of World War II and the passage of the G.I. Bill, college has become increasingly more important to getting the right job for you. In fact, if you missed college the first time

around (right after high school) you are, in all likelihood, relegated to a path in life with more limited opportunities for success.
The ever-worsening consequences of these barriers include unemployment, underemployment, and frustration with a world that, all
too often, is structured to reward only educational attainment. In
fact, the cruel truth is that today, as I write, it is estimated that
more than sixty million Americans have a high school degree and
some college credits, but no college degree. And many millions
more have graduated from high school but have no college experience at all.

One of the main elements of these barriers has been the refusal
of most colleges and employers to value the actual knowledge,
skills, and abilities that you have accumulated during your personal and work life—your "hidden credentials." Your hidden credentials are made up of *all* the learning you have done, throughout
your life, both inside and outside of school or college.

But like the tip of an iceberg, only the formal learning you have
accomplished as represented on a transcript or certificate is visible
and recognized by employers and colleges. Meanwhile the rest of
this iceberg of knowledge remains invisible to educators and employers. Thus the full value of your life experience—and the
knowledge it represents—lies concealed below the surface, out of
sight, out of mind, and without validation or recognition.

This is knowledge discrimination, pure and simple, because
what you know is valued based on where you learned it, not how
well you know it and can apply it. In this world, college-based learning is favored over job-based or life-based learning even if the college graduate has never had to actually "do" the work required.

To compound the problem, few of us are encouraged to understand and recognize that most of what we know has been learned
outside of schools and courses. With some estimates putting our
nonacademic learning at a significant majority of our total knowledge and ability, this is a practice that is personally damaging to
millions of people. Most universities and employers continue to

cling to traditional practices of favoring academic learning and training over a person's work experiences and direct life experiences. Finally, to add insult to this injury, very few of us are able to receive from others a proper appreciation of our skills and talents because we continue to keep them concealed.

But to quote Bob Dylan, "The times they are a-changin'." Remember in *The Wizard of Oz* when Toto the dog pulled the curtain back and unmasked the Wizard as "the little man in the corner pulling the levers"? Well, the same thing is happening with your hidden capabilities. Massive changes driven by the Digital Age have pulled back the curtain to expose the costs and unfairness of the tradition of colleges and employers failing to recognize the value of these credentials.

New programs and services that recognize and validate your actual knowledge, skills, and abilities are popping up in our life separate from our experiences with colleges and universities. As a result, colleges are increasingly being pressured to change their ways or suffer the consequences as learners go elsewhere for the recognition and validation that they need and deserve. These new services are also giving employers new ways to appraise and develop talent confidently without relying exclusively on academic degrees. Most importantly, these new services put you, the learner, in the driver's seat.

Free-Range Learning will help you to identify and value your hidden credentials, and in doing so, will enhance your sense of self-worth. This will help to link together your life experiences, learning, college or other training after high school, and your work in ways that more fully support and serve your needs and your purposes. You will *feel* better about what you have done and learned, and who you have become as a person, as you recognize your knowledge and growth. And you will *do* better by developing this awareness.

The "whole" of all your learning and life experiences is greater than the sum of their various parts. Discovering how to harness your hidden credentials becomes a dynamic process that will continue to enhance your success.

In *Free-Range Learning* you will read real stories of adults who have suffered from obstacles to learning and work that will help you understand what you can do about similar hurdles. The stories are about adults who found that they could learn useful knowledge and skills on their own and when armed with that knowledge they continued to learn new skills and find new opportunities.

Their descriptions of the turning points in their lives illustrate how they converted those times into positive transitions to greater career opportunities, additional learning experiences, and happier lives. Learning about their experiences will help you become more able to identify the crossroads in your life when you needed to make these transitions, and you may be at such a turning point right at this time.

You can also learn from the many examples given of how many barriers to success are coming down as new pathways are emerging. These factors are the "push" to the silent revolution in learning and work. This is the human need that has always been there, but which is now gaining voice, power, and momentum.

I describe this emerging ecosystem of new programs and services, including both collegiate and other opportunities, which are "friendly" to your circumstances, respectful of what you already know, and designed to help you:

- Meet your educational needs and achieve employment opportunities in the future.
- Bring your hidden credentials out of the closet and explore further learning opportunities through links to resources available through the worldwide web that support continued development. *This factor is the "pull" in the silent revolution—the new and emerging technologies that are liberating learning in the Digital Age.*

Free-Range Learning is a guide to help you begin a more conscious and purposeful learning journey. With increased realization of the capacities you have developed and appreciation for the learning you have already accomplished, you will be empowered to gain even more aptitudes in the future.

Section one of the book, "Understanding Your Personal Learning and Hidden Credentials," will introduce you to this reality of learning—the fact that you learn all the time. It describes its value and the great things that can happen when you harness and understand this personal learning from our experiences. For too long, we have been encouraged to ignore and devalue this kind of learning because it was not recognized or valued by colleges and employers. Through examples and interviews, you will see several of the ways that personal learning happens.

Chapter 1, "Hiding in Plain Sight," discusses the concept of the personal learning that informs your hidden credentials. I use examples of my own experience as well as the stories of other adults, in their own words, to define the idea clearly for you. It will help you to begin to understand your own personal learning and recognize its presence and impact on your life.

Chapter 2 describes turning points that are circumstances in your life that often drive your personal learning and the need to change. Events of divorce, loss of a job or frustration with work, the birth of a child, or death of a loved one can drive a change in your direction, attitude, or goals. As the stories from people I interviewed reveal, these crossroads in your life can involve a change in your behavior or alter the perception of your situation. You might decide you just need to change attitudes toward your work or might determine you need a new direction in life. It also shows how personal learning sometimes causes turning points that create the need for further learning and change.

The times when you are called upon to change in some important regard or suffer the consequences can trigger profound changes in your understanding of your goals. Often people who fail to respond well to the call for change become prisoners of their own experience, trapped in the circumstances of their reality. Others seize the moment and alter the course of their lives. Chapter 2 illustrates the positive results for people who enjoyed a successful conversion to a new direction in life, having come to a dramatic turning point and handled it successfully.

When you have finished the first section, you will have a clearer understanding of the validity and power of your personal learning and will be better able to identify some of its causes and consequences when you come to crisis points in your life. In section two I quote from the life stories of people I've interviewed to illustrate the many barriers—some apparent and others not easily discernable—that can frustrate your access to the learning you need and the career you want. Of course, sometimes we are our own worst enemies when it comes to erecting barriers to progress. But chapters 3 and 4 will help you understand that in many cases isolation from learning opportunities is not all your fault or a sign of weakness. Just as importantly, you will see that you are not alone!

I remember seeing a holiday image years ago that has stayed with me ever since. You may remember it. It is a picture of two children looking longingly through a store window at cakes and pies that they cannot afford. They were so near, and yet so far from what they wanted. In the same vein, you may have often wondered, "How did my life get so complicated?" Or "Why is college so remote and difficult for me to negotiate?" Or "Why is identifying and preparing for a new job, let alone getting one, so difficult?"

"Unfriendly" college practices and bewildering job requirements and application processes are common barriers to many adults. And, frankly, too many employers' biases about qualifications and education play a negative role as well. In too many cases "who" you know and where you went to school is more important that "what" you know and how well you can apply it. This is "knowledge discrimination" pure and simple. You are being penalized based on where and how you did your learning, not rewarded and recognized for what you know and can do.

The good news, however, is that those barriers are coming down. New services now employ practices that use evidence of your hidden credentials to qualify you as a job applicant. Using free-range learning resources, you and your skills and knowledge will no longer be left out in the cold as you aspire to learn more to have a better or different job to improve your life.

Chapter 3, "The Scarecrow's Dilemma," describes other adults' experiences when trying to get access to college and, in one case, weathering the college experience once admitted. It gives examples of policies and practices, including ignoring your hidden credentials, which frustrate adult learners and send the message that college is not meant for them. The "college gap" can be partially psychological. Some people are raised to believe that going to college is not part of their future. But, as this section will show, the gap is also caused by college traditions and practices that are simply not "adult-friendly' and which make the path to success steeper and more challenging.

In chapter 4, "Adult-Friendly Colleges," I profile the pioneering exemplary colleges and universities that are already adapting to adult learners and their needs and respect the learning and knowledge that the adults bring with them, wherever it was gained. Some of these colleges may be right next door to you, while programs of others may be online and in different states. But what they all have in common are policies and practices that put you, the learner, and your hidden credentials at the head of the class. The stories of graduates will illuminate these colleges' visions and intentions as they break the old mold of higher education. And they will help you recognize the elements of "adult-friendly colleges" to aid you in your selection.

Then, in chapter 5, "Adult-Friendly College Presidents Speak: What You have a Right to Expect from College and Why," five presidents of this new breed of college describe the services they offer that distinguish them from most other colleges. To be fair, there are several other colleges that do some or perhaps all of these things. These are identified later in the book so that you can learn about them as well.

By the end of section two, you will be able to identify the obstacles that have frustrated you and kept you from the education and jobs that you want. And the gap between your abilities and getting value for your learning and work will have been humanized and personalized through real stories told in the words of real people. You will also, however, have gotten a taste of what you deserve, the new possibilities and services that the digital age is bringing to you as a "free-range learner."

And then we will turn to the present and the future as I examine in some detail some examples of the new services that are empowering learners by bringing down barriers and costs to education and work, while improving personalization and quality.

The chapters in section three, "The Emerging GPS for Learning and Work," describe the emerging ecosystem of new practices that put you in the driver's seat by encouraging "free-range learning" in our Digital Age. I will introduce you to several categories of programs and services, some very new and others more established, which can help you plan and execute your learning journey and strengthen your hidden credentials. Importantly, the chapters will give you the electronic connections to these services and institutions.

You will see firsthand what these new services and programs can do for you from the experiences described during my interviews with learners. By the time you finish section three, you will have access to tools and resources which help you successfully plan your future learning path. These will help you to deepen and add value to your hidden credentials as you dynamically link your life experience, informal learning, college, and work into a plan for the future.

Chapter 6, "Cracking the Code: Getting to the Right College or Credentials," introduces you to services and organizations that will specifically help you do the following:

- Find the right college "fit" for you
- Identify adult-friendly colleges around the country
- Estimate the value of your experiential learning and hidden credentials
- Identify the academic value of corporate, labor, military, or other courses you have taken during your life

This will continue to help you to identify and describe the value of your hidden credentials. This can be very frustrating because, in many cases, feeling ready to become a college graduate and being ready to work effectively are two entirely different things. And, while graduates get the jobs, your inability to get to college or get through college or find other avenues to validate your learning has made getting the work you want almost impossible.

Chapter 7, "Getting the Skills You Need," introduces you to revolutionary new services and pathways that are entering this job training area. In this new and developing ecosystem, you can further develop your personal learning and hidden credentials and bring them directly into play as significant assets in the job-search game. And, importantly, much of the knowledge gained through personal learning experience—behavioral traits such as teamwork and intellectual skill sets such as critical thinking—are considered vital to job success, but have been largely ignored in collegiate settings and as employment qualifications. In short, as you use these new pathways, your hidden credentials that have often been ignored by academics and employers will be on the table as viable and significant assets.

I also describe several newly existing services which offer courses, sequences of learning, and micro-credentials at no or very low cost. These resources can also connect you to other colleges and organizations sympathetic to your learning. Your personal learning is the focus in this chapter. On the one hand, learning is a social activity, and most people like to learn in a group and under the sponsorship of a college, an employer, or another formal, external entity. On the other hand, if your purpose is to simply "Do It Yourself," this chapter will encourage you to go out on your own, chart your own learning path, and do it yourself.

The new businesses and organizations you will learn about in chapter 7 are emblematic of many other services that are beginning to populate the landscape of employers and adult learners. They are just examples of what is happening in our Digital Age. And each provides a clear example of an option that did not exist ten years ago while having its value described in the words of a learner as the walls between learning in our daily life, career, and college are coming down.

Happily, in the "free-range learning" world, the same services can serve individuals as well as institutions and employers. You set the conditions and the terms for how you participate and with whom.

You can quickly see how this emerging ecosystem for learning and work supports you and your learning experience, whether it is DIY or connected to college or career.

In chapter 8, I introduce you to a few new tools and services that can support your success in new learning and work ventures. They will be helpful in several ways. For example, if a college you are considering is employing one or more of these services, such as Portfolium, Civitas, or HelioCampus, it can be an indicator of enhanced "adult-friendliness." Or, if you are a returning veteran, you might use COOL to help you link your military learning to existing civilian jobs.

You will quickly come to understand the value of these new services. They offer assessments of your behavior and attitudes and an analysis of your strengths and skills to help you determine which learning experiences and programs will enhance your job readiness. These services also provide tools and data bases to help you to identify and connect with employers who might be interested in giving you recognition for your life-learning experiences.

Finally, in chapter 9, I present discussions of the ideas of some of the leading innovators and entrepreneurs who are driving all this disruptive change. When "the Innovators Speak," you will learn of their empowering and invigorating vision for the world that is opening up for learning and work. It will help you to form your own expectations for this new world and this emerging GPS (Global Positioning System) for learning and work. This is critically important because, in this world, you are the driver!

Free-Range Learning will give you the stories, information, examples, connections, and tools needed to blaze your own learning trail to the future you want. Let's get started.

FREE-RANGE LEARNING IN THE DIGITAL AGE

UNDERSTANDING YOUR PERSONAL LEARNING AND HIDDEN CREDENTIALS

1

HIDING IN PLAIN SIGHT
RECOGNIZING YOUR
PERSONAL LEARNING

PERSONAL LEARNING HAS TWO ASPECTS. It can result in the actual acquisition of new knowledge and concrete skills. It can also reveal changes in your attitudes and behavior as you continually grow, change, and become another person. Both aspects are important elements in your personal, social, civic, and career success. All too often, however, we ignore or forget our personal learning.

Personal learning comes in all shapes, sizes, and containers. It has no uniform model. For example, I remember a day in the mid-1980s when I was sorting through old photographs. It was one of those lazy Sunday afternoon jobs saved for a winter weekend. I came across a picture of me cradling one of my sons, taken at least a dozen years earlier, when I was still president of the Community College of Vermont.

As I looked at the smiling person holding the infant in the photo, I realized with a physical shock that I was looking at a stranger, a person who no longer existed. This was not the face that I saw in the mirror each morning when I shaved. This was someone much younger, insulated by his own naiveté, mostly un-scarred and unseasoned. The man I was looking at in the picture had not known failure in business, had not suffered defeat in politics. In the ensuing twelve years, I had developed and evolved into a different version of Peter Smith.

The events of the intervening years had rushed by: my father's death, becoming a father for the third time, elections won and lost, and serving in statewide constitutional office. It was dizzying. There was a chasm of unreflected experience between the man in the picture and the person I had become.

Looking at the stranger in the photograph, I realized that a river of learning and change had flowed through me that required some consideration. For whatever reasons, and there were many at play that Sunday afternoon—some glaringly public and others intensely personal—the shock of seeing myself as a person other than who I had understood myself to be demanded my attention. I realized that I had grown away from the earlier version and had become, for better or for worse, a new and more nuanced person. And I had to get to know him better.[1]

Over time, this realization led me to multiple conversations with friends and family members, reading about transitions in life, and an increased sensitivity to the daily events in my life. Ultimately, I reached a clearer understanding of who I had become. Importantly, I came to understand that this kind of personal growth and change continued throughout life.

There are two significant things to know about your personal learning. First, it happens continually throughout your life. And second, as happened with me, most of us are routinely unaware of this powerful source of change in our lives, diminishing its value.

Just how much learning you regularly accomplish was described by Allen Tough in *The Adult's Personal Learning Projects*:[2]

Almost everyone undertakes at least one or two major learning projects a year. Some people undertake as many as fifteen or twenty. The median is eight projects a year lasting a total of eight hundred hours. (*author's note*: That is fifteen hours a week you may be spending in learning!)

If you are like most people, you haven't seriously considered the possibility that you have achieved significant personal learning, let alone tried to put a value on it. But it is there throughout your life, constituting an iceberg of knowledge, but only revealing tips of ability while leaving the larger body of knowledge and ability hidden beneath the surface. If you do not understand and value your experience and the learning it contains, you can be imprisoned by it, unconscious of its influence on your worldview, your skills, and your knowledge. Losing track of your personal learning and its value means losing track of who you are becoming and why.

Highly deliberate learning efforts take place all around you. The members of your family, your neighbors, colleagues, and acquaintances probably initiate and complete several learning efforts every year. . . . *[italics added] But interestingly . . . when asked about their learning efforts, many of our interviewees recalled none at first. As the interviews proceeded, however, they recalled several recent efforts to learn.*

The act of being reminded of and recalling your personal learning is a life-changing event, because coming to terms with the personal changes that your accumulation of knowledge through experience inevitably causes several things to happen. You become more self-confident and assured. And, in the future, you will go through more conscious and deliberate transitions of age and development. When you learn to keep track of your learning, you can begin to have an effect on your personal and career development in a deliberate way by recognizing and integrating changes as they occur. Then a transition in life reaffirms and clarifies your learning and strengthens your capacity to learn in the future.

Stunning affirmation of this fact first came to me at the first graduation of the Community College of Vermont (CCV) in the mid-1970s. I was presiding over the ceremony as the founding president of the college. CCV worked with students to recognize the knowledge they brought with them, believing that making people relearn what they already knew was neither practical nor fair. It was a radical thought in those days, but it worked. One graduate, a woman named Nancy Burns who ran her own childcare center, came up to me and said, "The programs were great, and thank you for them. But my greatest thanks is for helping me see how much I had learned outside of school, how much it was worth, and what kind of a person I have become. Now I know I'm a learner, and I'll never stop learning!"[3]

Another man had learned public speaking as the head of a local volunteer agency. And a fellow student had managed her own business for ten years, learning from her experiences, her peers, and her reading throughout. They had both devalued and "forgotten" that knowledge until it was called out by the college's assessment of prior experiential learning. Coming to see the value of this filled these individuals with pride as well as a sense of increased self-worth and confidence. Their learning was "hiding in plain sight." It only had to be recalled and valued.

And there was a powerful piece of of learning experience for me that day as well. I began to see that understanding and valuing personal and experiential learning was more than a book-keeping practice, an issue of fairness and efficiency to get adult learners more academic credit. I began to understand that the assessment process itself was deeply educational in its own right, that it was a teaching and learning tool which encouraged personal and professional development in a way that most college classes or workplace training programs did not. In short, I came to understand that deep thinking about what you have learned from a specific experience, be it a course, a job, or a personal event, was in and of itself a form of learning. And being asked to reflect on and weigh its value was a form of teaching.

All of this recently discovered reality affirms the mythology of opportunity that is laced throughout American folklore. This mythology, expressed through phrases and stories, is the keystone to the American Dream, delivering its message again and again.

Live and Learn
The School of Hard Knocks
Older, but Wiser
From Rags to Riches

In each case, the message is similar. You can learn from the experience of living. There are strong and useful connections between effort, learning, and success. We believe deeply that if you are resourceful, work hard, and learn on your feet, opportunity will come knocking.

Part of the mythology is correct. As Allen Tough found, people do learn actively and purposefully all the time. In fact, the median adult spends about fifteen hours every week on highly specific learning projects. And colleges account for only a small portion of all that learning.

But what the mythology covers up is the deep-seated knowledge discrimination that occurs when it comes to college and jobs. That's right, knowledge discrimination. Since most of your personal learning is done away from colleges, it is valued less, indeed ignored, when it comes to college credit and career access.

Consider the sources of this powerful, if disrespected learning. You are learning when:

- You look at videos on Facebook about child development and discuss parenting with a friend in order to cope better with the children in your life;
- Your supervisor at work demonstrates a new technique or the company brings in a presenter to describe a new technological or process development;
- You develop a health and diet plan to keep more physically fit while eating well;
- You learn how to use a new computer program at work;

- You read books, view podcasts, or surf the web on China or Mexico to know more about those countries or to plan a trip;
- You study investment practices and then practice with your investments in order to make more with the small amount you have laid aside; or
- You learn to play an instrument, engage in therapy, or learn a new sport.

Your personal learning has three important characteristics.

- *It is personal.* You usually learn alone or in small groups in an informal setting.
- *It is purposeful.* You always learn for a reason, even if you forget the reason or consider the learning inconsequential. As a result, much of the learning is absorbed into your collective experience and forgotten.
- *It is powerful.* Personal learning is continually changing you, developing your behavior, skills, knowledge, and attitudes into a set of hidden credentials. Often, however, you fail to think about what you've learned and how you have changed.[4]

Now, let's hear the stories of several adult learners who have come to grips with their personal learning. When I spoke with her in Montpelier, Vermont, Carol Harrison confirmed that she had had similar experiences with personal learning and change, although she came by them in very different ways.

▶ Carol Harrison

Carol Harrison, Director of Finance and Logistics for the Department of Motor Vehicles at the State of Vermont, is a direct, intelligent woman with a penetrating gaze. She described a very different journey from mine and how she came to understand that journey and its value to her.

"I've had an amazing ride. As a first-born of European immigrants, college was not in the cards for me as a young woman. I had no confidence that I could or should go to college and get a degree. It just wasn't in the cards. Looking back on it all, you might say that it took me a while to become my own best friend when it came to learning and college.

As things turned out, I got married and began what turned into a multiple-year odyssey as I traveled with my husband to multiple military assignments in the US and Europe. Without consciously focusing on it, I began to accumulate experiences and college courses somewhat randomly along the way.

I took my first college course in central Texas with my husband. We did it together. I completed with an 'A' and he got a 'B.' (she chuckles.) Eventually we moved to El Paso where I attended EL Paso Community College, supported by a Texas state military tuition program. I received an Associate's Degree in General Management. I loved the community college environment because of the diversity in the classroom. The people I was learning with came from all over the United States and had an incredible variety of experiences to share. This was an "invisible" factor and not intentionally part of the course. But it added greatly to the overall value of the learning experience.

I also supported my husband as he earned his master's degree by going to the library to get articles and do research. Doing these things, I learned a lot just by looking over his shoulder and supporting him along the way. Even today, I value how much I learn from others. It may be incidental learning because I am not the main focus. But it is powerful and valuable learning as well.

Then we went to Germany where, in retrospect, I can see that my learning continued along two different lines. I took a few language courses at the University of Maryland University College (UMUC) at one of their remote campus locations on a military base. It was a great experience because, once again, I got the community of the classroom along with the support of a military program. But I was also learning about language and culture, and that was very important to me at the time.

At the same time, I had my adventurous spirit going for me, and I immersed myself in the German culture. I lived in the community, became friends with my German neighbors, attended nearby cultural events, learned to speak the slang dialogue of the region where I lived, took a cooking course from a local farmer's wife, and even picked up a few German cuss words along the way.

Blending in with my new cultural surroundings was a learning experience that can't be found in any classroom. Learning and using the language deepened the experience. For instance, there are many ways to greet people throughout Germany. And saying "good morning" in Bavaria is quite different than saying it in Hessen. Each region has its own nuances and subcultures which added richness to every new experience.

I've had an amazing journey with all sorts of personal and professional experiences that made all the difference in the world. Because of moving so frequently in the military, I needed a plan of action which included re-inventing myself every three or four years. That led to conscious lifelong and continuous learning decisions. My travels over sixteen years, attending nine colleges and universities in two countries and several states, ultimately led to my earning a master's degree. All that learning, personal and formal, paid off.

As I look back, I think it was actually good for me to first take a little time to see and experience some of what life had to offer. This time gave me a chance to learn my own true desires, discover my aptitudes, and head in a direction all my own. For example, recently I took Gallup's Clifton Strength-Finders assessments (www.gallupstrenghtscenter.com), and it described me as:

- A responsible leader
- A person of deliberate action
- A relator with people
- A constant learner
- One who maximizes results.

I like these descriptions and find them to be quite accurate. They have contributed to and been strengthened by all the experiences I have had in my life."

What a story! In it you see a woman taking advantage of her life journey to, as she put it, benefit not only from the colleges she encountered, but also from all of the learning experiences that existed in the community around her, including helping her husband in his academic work. All the while she is collecting knowledge and experience. And, more recently, she has become more aware of her on-going, current personal learning, a very empowering turn of events.

▶ Connie Yu Naylor

When I spoke with Connie, she had worked on three continents in six jobs over a fifteen-year period. Clearly a bright woman, Connie still felt, in her own terms, . . . "like a chip of wood carried on the water. Not very smart, just a hard worker."

"When I first came to America, I really didn't like myself at all because here I am, a strange creature in a country of people who all know what they're doing. Not only had I not gone to college, but I began to realize that there were things that mattered to me that didn't seem to matter to most people around me. I was very lonely, and I had to decide either to try to reach people, to communicate, or go back where I belonged. Finally, I thought, 'I'm here. This is my life. I must reach these people.

Well, first I tried to read people's minds. But how do you read people's minds without understanding what makes them feel, what made them become what they are? There are mental thought patterns that are different—your philosophy and history. I went back to American philosophy because I wanted to understand, to discover the American instinct. And I started reading many books on your history and culture, and on Western interpretations of Eastern meditation to see how your world tries to understand mine.

Now I am becoming aware of the riches of the people around me. It's like discovering souls, lost dimensions in people. And the more I'm beginning to understand and reach people, the more I am giving of myself. I think it flows together, like a link. I'm feeling better and better about myself.

And I'm surprised at all the things that I have learned that I wasn't thinking about. Initially, I didn't realize that I wanted to learn American philosophy because I was lonely. I thought it was, you know, a seeking of knowledge. But there's always a reason why you learn, isn't there? Why was I feeling sorry for myself? I've done a lot. I'm suddenly very aware of where I am and what my expectations are.

In the beginning here, I thought I was just a silly female, not very smart, but a hard worker. Now people are beginning to listen to what I say. I'm beginning to realize, 'Hey, I have something to offer'—that I am, you know, someone who can take my role and my part in this world. I'm suddenly comfortable with people whom I was very uncomfortable with before because I thought they knew what I didn't know. Now I know we're even.

Now, as I'm having some of this success, I am finding that the income measurement is not as important to me. I'm beginning to think, you know, "What really counts? Is it important for me to keep working to get up there, up that wealth ladder? Or is it important to me just to survive and develop myself as a person?"

Remember Allen Tough's findings mentioned earlier in this chapter. When first asked, most people were not able to recall even recent learning they had accomplished. It was only when the interviewer began to ask them probing questions that they recalled their learning.

Carol and Connie Yu's personal learning was "hiding in plain sight." They might have remembered some of the events in their lives. But they needed a special event, a new pair of glasses, to see and understand their personal learning and its importance. And it was only when they looked back on life that the true, deeper value of their personal learning became apparent. Indeed, it is this later, after the fact reflection that develops the "habit" of understanding your personal learning and extracting meaning from your lived experience. And once you get the knack of it, you never lose that ability. In my experience, your ability to learn more thoroughly through reflection only deepens with time.

Let's explore now in chapter two the other two important elements in personal learning, turning points in life and the transitions that can occur after you come to a turning point. Personal learning as you interact with life circumstances can and will bring you to turning points. And, in turn, they can lead to a new and different future if you harness them correctly.

Remember the three P's of personal learning—personal, purposeful, and powerful. And remember the power of claiming and understanding your personal learning so you can develop your hidden credentials. As you will see, "free-range learning in the Digital Age" is ushering in a time when personal learning and your hidden credentials will be honored and valued in college and at work.

Then, in chapters three and four we will explore the barriers to college that have existed for adult learners for years and present some powerful examples of solutions that have been developed through new institutional forms. There have been many obstacles. Some are personally imposed, others are institutional. But at their heart is the historic inability to harness the academic and economic power of peoples' personal learning, the kind of learning you heard about from Carolyn and Connie. Collectively, these practices have kept people "on the outside looking in" when it came to college and prevented them "getting from here to there" when looking for a job.

2

TURNING POINTS AND TRANSITIONS

WHETHER OR NOT YOU ARE aware of your personal learning as it happens, at some point you recognize that you have changed over the years. This recognition can range from a casual observation of the characteristics of aging to more profound understandings of growth, aspirations, and opportunities in your professional development.

Although turning points that involve personal learning are profound, they are also a consequence of time passing. Facing a crossroads in your life can mean the most to you if it initiates the following progression of events:

- You realize that you need to change the course of your life, that past assumptions no longer make sense, that a new perception and understanding of yourself is affecting you, and you must come to grips with it. You reappraise yourself.
- You gain confidence and a sense of self-worth as you take stock of your personal learning and become aware of the skills, abilities, and values that you have gained over the years.

- And, with your increased ability to reflect on your learning, you become a conscious learner, anticipating future transitions and enhancing your life with continuous and purposeful learning.

- Approaching a turning point in your life can be triggered by a crisis —a lost job, a divorce, or an illness in the family—or by a positive event that spurs you on, like your child going to college when you did not. The key question, however, is how will you react as you approach the crossroads. Will you fail to grasp it? Will it overwhelm you? Will it be a wrenching experience that leaves you looking at a stranger in the mirror, wondering who you have become? Or, can you convert it into a moment of learning and self-realization that changes the way you see the world, stimulating more learning that augments what you already know?[5]

I have had several such moments in my life—times when I simply had to choose a direction and the consequences were big. Two come to mind as I write today.

While I was studying education in graduate school, I wrestled, as did most of my fellow students, with the issue of where I would begin my professional life. And the answer throughout that fall was Alaska. After all, I had traveled and worked there twice, and my sister Susan lived there with her family (still does, in fact). And it was far away, romantic, and very rugged, which fit my Outward Bound and National Outdoor Leadership School (NOLS) experiences.

In spite of this, I had a persistent, gnawing sense that I was running away from something—that there was a "push" as well as a "pull" in my calculations. Why didn't I want to go to Vermont where I knew so many people, the terrain, and the history so well? And then, one sunny Sunday afternoon in North Cambridge, it hit me: I was afraid to go to Vermont.

My extended family was large and had played a significant role in the political and economic development of the state (particularly northwestern Vermont) since their arrival around 1800. The "push" towards Alaska was my fear that I would not be able to develop my own professional and social identity under this historic "cloud" of family achievement. I was afraid that, both in terms of career arc and psychologically, it would control me.

I struggled with this fear all afternoon that day. It was a little like wrestling an elusive greased pig: furtive, dodging in and out of the shadows of my consciousness; being denied, then affirmed, and finally . . . understood. I reckoned with it and the message was clear.

It went like this: *Peter, you cannot run away from your family name and history or the privilege, the responsibility, and the identity that comes with it. You could be in Madrid, Spain, get robbed and left for dead in an alley. And, if you could beg a dime and get to a phone, you could call home and everything would be okay. Also, if your family can dominate you in Vermont, they can dominate you wherever you are. The fear you have is your construction, not theirs. You can either deal with it or it will color your life. Decide where you want to live and go there. And, no matter what, understand your privilege and what you are going to do to be yourself, and use it for good things, if you can.*

I went to Vermont, and over the next twenty years I lived near and loved my parents, siblings, cousins, aunts, and uncles. And I charted my own path, sometimes to their consternation. During that time, I founded the state's community college system (Community College of Vermont) and served as a state senator, Lieutenant Governor, and Congressman-at-Large before leaving the Congress in 1990 at the age of forty-five. Going to Vermont began a transition to a productive and fulfilling professional and personal life.

In the end, everything worked out for the best. But without the turning point I experienced that sunny Sunday afternoon in North Cambridge, I am not sure any of that would have happened.

Twenty years later, I had another Vermont-related turning point. This time it had to do with staying or leaving. I had lost my seat in the United States Congress and was having trouble getting a job that I wanted in Vermont. It seemed a good time to visit a friend, confidant, and advisor, Sister Janice Ryan, in her president's office of Trinity College in Burlington, Vermont.

I had come to know Sister Janice Ryan and her dear friend, Sister Elizabeth Candon, when I was starting the Community College of Vermont. She was Vice-President of Academic Affairs at Trinity College and then, subsequently, became the president. Sister Janice had done many brave things, including being a crusader against land mines and other global issues. She had been a mentor to me throughout my career.

Sister Janice helped me see my way down one of the toughest paths I have ever had to follow: deciding what to do when I left the Congress in 1991.

I had determined that making yet another political comeback was not in the cards. After all, I had been at it for twelve years, winning four races, but losing three. My reasoning was as follows: If you bat .570 in baseball, you go to the Hall of Fame. But if you bat .570 in politics, you need to find another line of work!

And I had determined that higher education and helping previously marginalized people learn things that mattered, was where my heart and my passion lay.

I had also decided that as much as I respected other occupations I had considered, I was simply not cut out to be in the insurance or real estate fields. There were opportunities in each that would keep me in Vermont, but they just weren't for me.

At the same time, the leadership opportunities available to me in Vermont higher education in Vermont appeared to range from limited to nonexistent. Furthermore, my eight year battle to found and institutionalize the Community College of Vermont had, as Sister Janice would confirm, earned me some long-term skeptics and a few downright enemies. An in-state college presidency had just eluded me, and I found myself in Sister Janice's office at Trinity, looking for advice.

She listened carefully as I laid out my situation, walking through the points I had analyzed, but still looking for direction. Then, very gently, she asked me whether I wanted to be president of one or two Vermont colleges that were new and in need of leadership. I answered, "No. I have done that already here. I need something more." Sister Janice sighed and said, "Then you are going to have to leave Vermont. Maybe you will come back, maybe you will not. But the future you are seeking is not here right now."

I sat in her office, tears in my eyes, as the truth of what she had said sunk in.

At that moment, however, the second half of my professional and personal life was born. It would be a life away from the Vermont I loved. But it has also been a life full of richness and challenge that has taken me across the country and around the world in my ongoing love affair with learning. And Sister Janice, my friend and mentor, was the one who showed me the way.

Both of these turning points were intensely personal. And in each case, my self-confidence and sense of self-worth were tested as I faced the challenge ahead.

Other crossroads, while less dramatic are nonetheless critically important. Handling a turning point in your life positively hinges on a realization of self-worth that comes with the recognition of knowledge and attitudes that have been learned over the years. Sometimes that learning is from personal experiences involving your behavior, values, and relationships with other people. At other times it is career-based and related to your knowledge, skills, abilities, and opportunities at work. Either way, handling a turning-point experience positively includes a significant change in your perception of yourself and an improved sense of your self-worth. But first, you have to face the facts.

▶ Elaine McDermott

Elaine McDermott is a great example of a person who very unexpectedly came to a turning point in her life and struggled with the challenge. Elaine was a math teacher before she raised her two daughters. She had always planned to return to teaching when her children were in school. However, a confusing and agonizing turning point stimulated new insights and led Elaine to make a very different decision about her career.

"For years I had been thinking that when the girls were in school I would go back to teaching. That first year I took a temporary job at a local coin company running their retail store. I was planning to apply for teaching jobs for the following fall. My whole attitude about running the store was that this was fun. I would try it for a while. I knew I wasn't growing. It was just bucks and it was boring, but it was nice to get out and be earning. I kept telling people that I was just doing it for now, until I could get a job in June teaching. Because I wasn't growing, I wasn't learning anything. I thought I had control over it. Then they took it all away from me on New Year's Eve.

There had been two major layoffs before then so the writing was on the wall. But I still thought I had a couple of months if it was going to be their choice. If it was going to be mine, I had until June. I didn't foresee that my job was going to end in December.

I can't identify the feeling that I felt at the time. We went out and had drinks and laughed, but it was just . . . there was a strange atmosphere because you were making believe you were happy about something when you really weren't. I was really going to miss the money, and it called my bluff about other jobs.

I was sort of in a state of shock for three weeks. That may sound like a strong statement, but I think I was, because, as I look back on it, I couldn't identify what was going on at the time. I was staying home saying, 'Isn't this wonderful, I can spend all day reading.' But it was awful. And I couldn't recognize that. After about a month, I identified the anger, which was good. But then, the depression hit, and I thought, 'My God, what am I going to do? My kids are in school, and I'm thirty-five years old, and I've got to get my act together.'

I had a friend who was going through a divorce—not by her choice. She was the victim, and she was going through a lot of things that a lot of women go through who made a career of following their husbands around and haven't established anything for themselves. I thought about what she was going through, and I thought that if I didn't find something, if I didn't get my act together, I could be that same woman.

So I said, 'Okay, you can't wait until June anymore. Now, what are you going to do?' Well, I was going to teach because that had been my pat answer for the past ten years. So, I started sending resumes to area schools. Then I started getting replies. That was the thing that threw me into another depression, because, at that point I had to make a commitment. Writing the letters was no commitment.

I realized that I didn't want to teach anymore. It was just something that I hadn't thought about for ten years. I always felt that that was what I would do when the kids were grown. Plus, George was encouraging me, too—which he would do because he had been listening to me for all those years and here I was, applying for these school jobs, so why wouldn't he think that. But I heard him on the phone one night, telling his parents that I was going to teach. And hearing it as a third party, all of a sudden I said, 'Wait a minute. That's not me. I don't think I'm going to do that. No, I'm not going to do that.'"

During those years at home, Elaine's life had changed outwardly. But she wasn't aware of a corresponding inner change in her personal aspirations and expectations. They had changed so slowly that she continued to carry a clear but outdated image of herself as a teacher when she returned to work. It wasn't until circumstances gave her no alternative that Elaine confronted the changes in herself. She became more aware of her values. She didn't want to teach.

It took Elaine ten years to reach her turning point, even though she had been changing the entire time. A deeper self-awareness was necessary to complete the changes as the decision loomed before her. Only then did she decide to seek further training and become a paralegal, thus further deepening her self-awareness.

"I had always been interested in the law. At one point, I had regretted that I hadn't done something in the law when I got out of college. I had heard of a local school that trained paralegals, but I just kind of filed it. Every now and then I'd bring it up with people when I thought I still had a choice. But it was just a faint consideration, in the back of my mind.

I was just not knowing what I was going to do. Then I heard there was an orientation meeting at the paralegal school the following Thursday and I thought, 'Maybe that's what I need, right now.' So I gave them a call and told them I'd be there. That just unlocked something. It cemented the decision and my resolve to go. I felt as if I had made a commitment to do something that had been in me for a long time. I sat down that day and wrote two letters, one to my in-laws and one to a friend, and I told them that I was going to paralegal school."

Her turning point brought her to a crossroads in her aspirations for future work. As difficult as approaching that crossroads was, Elaine ultimately seized it as an opportunity and put the learning it generated to work for her. Elaine learned self-awareness and gained insight into her motives and aspirations when she finally confronted the consequences of being laid off. Then, she grappled with the powerlessness that comes from a lack of direction and chose a new course for her life. It was a transition well-navigated.

▶ Kelley Lawrence

Kelley was learning how to live on her own after her divorce. And she was working while also raising her young son. She was, in her own words, "coping" with the hand that life had dealt her, trying to provide a decent quality of life for them both. And then came the lightning bolt that changed her course.

> "There I was: twenty-nine years old, newly divorced, with a young son at home. One day we were taking a drive, and we got to talking about what he wanted to do when he grew up. He told me that he wanted to be a marine biologist, but that he was not going to go to college because neither of his parents had gone to college.
>
> I was the first person in my family to be born in America. And I would have been the first child going off to college. I just thought at the time that I wasn't ready. I wasn't ready to leave home. It just wasn't the right time. But ten years later, this event changed everything. I didn't want my son to not go to college because neither his dad nor I went. I took it personally to set an example so he couldn't use it as an excuse. That was the crossroads moment for me.
>
> So that was it. I went home that night and looked up Community College of Vermont courses. And the next day I spoke with my employer and she helped get me connected. There was no way I was going to let the example I set define and determine my son's aspirations.
>
> By the way (and Kelley smiles broadly), my son is almost ready for college. He wants to be an aeronautical engineer. I am very proud of him and of what I have done."

▶ *Aaron Roberts*

For Aaron, the path was very different. In his own words, he had an "epic battle" with his career.

> "I went to college in 1986. I had a huge attitude, a chip on my shoulder. I wanted to show that my way was right and the best way every time. Before I knew it, I was on academic probation and out the door.

For the next ten to twelve years, I had an epic battle with my career. I did all sorts of things. I was a plumbing apprentice and an HVAC installer. I did commercial cleaning, and I sold appliances. I even sold life insurance for a while. I was way too smart for myself.

In 2000, I was hired by Comcast Cable as a cable installer technician. I did well at work, starting as a technician and then moving up into management. But one day I realized that I was not satisfied with my role and responsibilities. At the same time, it dawned on me that I needed new tools and resources to develop and create the future state I desired. I am smart, but I didn't have the degree. And, you know, you need it to move ahead. And even though I thought I knew a lot, I also thought that maybe I wasn't as good as I thought I was. Maybe there were some things I needed to know that I hadn't learned on my own. That was the turning point for me. I thought, 'This is it, buddy. Either buckle down and do it or nothing's going to change.'

My HR director at Comcast put me in touch with a college that would assess my prior learning and that was that. It changed my world and my perspective about learning. Now I am open to the fact that I learn every day. My motto has become *Question what you feel and challenge what you know every day.* Understanding the personal learning that I have done, here's how I would summarize from my experiences:

- Set your personal goal for your educational future.
- Know that it's a journey, not a race.
- Be sure that every step you take moves you towards that goal.
- Keep track of all those steps, because they add up to your future success."

▶ *Jennifer Carr*

Jennifer was plenty smart, but college just didn't grab her attention the way she thought it would. So she went in some other directions for several years.

"I went to college straight out of high school, but I didn't know what I wanted to do with my academic studies. I think this is a problem for many young people. If you don't know where you are going and why, college can be uninspiring.

So, for me, I ultimately left college because I got interested in environmental issues. I went to work for Greenpeace and got engaged with issues about which I was passionate. But I couldn't relate the things I was learning to the academic world. And I found that I was learning more about the political and systemic roots of environmental problems through my activist, hands-on work. I stayed at Greenpeace, and I ended up with a position in the major gifts program. Over time, that led to other jobs in the nonprofit world that broadened my body of experience.

As time passed, however, I began to sense that if I had to get a job more formally, I was overqualified from my experience but underqualified on paper. Putting it bluntly, once I realized that, it made my future prospects look professionally unsatisfying.

Then, while I was working at a position on Marlboro College's development team, I was able to take a one-semester class where I earned a Certificate in Non-Profit Management through the School of Graduate and Professional Studies. I found the experience to be enjoyable and rewarding. But it also showed me that other people, people who sometimes had less experience than I had, but people who had college degrees were able to advance more easily into leadership positions.

That was that. I knew that I had to finish my undergraduate education and get the degree if I was going to get the kind of work that I wanted and was capable of doing.

One of the most inspiring things about returning to school was meeting the other adults in the program and becoming aware of the amazing work each was doing. I was blown away by the substantive work they had done before and during their time in the program. It made me realize that there is no one real profile of a person who didn't finish college the first time around. Also, you can't make assumptions about why some people don't earn college degrees right out of high school. This deepened my respect for the quality of learning that goes on in each of our daily lives.

As I looked into what it would take to finish, I learned about the Assessment of Prior Learning course and the External Bachelors program at Johnson State College. I was certain that I had a lot to gain from getting credit in APL, including saving time and money as I earned the degree. Another big thing was that the assessment allowed me to avoid taking courses in subjects that I already knew.

I gained a lot from the assessment process. I was amazingly affirmed when my former colleagues and employers were willing to step up for me, testifying and documenting my skills and abilities. It also forced me to put my experiences in story form, to sort of sit back and reflect and better understand my career path. It made me feel more intentional about the things I had done, and it was very motivating to have my experience confirmed with academic credentials.

I graduated in May 2017. And, while this did not create an instant dramatic change in my life, I am positioned to move forward when I need to because of my learning and the degree. So I have the confidence that I lacked before because I have been 'qualified' in a way that I wasn't before. It is a very different feeling. The experience, coupled with the right degree, make me less vulnerable to situations that are out of my control that could force me to make an unexpected career change. I am more self-assured than I was. It's a great feeling."

Although personal learning can have a dramatic effect, it is often difficult to recognize because it accumulates one bit at a time, like snow falling, one flake at a time. Recognizing the learning is difficult enough to do. But learning to evaluate it, harness its value, and use it consciously in your personal and professional development are the crucial next steps. When you can do that, many wrenching "crossroads events" such as the one faced by Elaine can be converted into smoother successful transitions as you chart your new path forward.

Personal crises like the one that Elaine faced at her turning point can either lead to chaos or improvements. Like a slap in the face, they can force you to reckon with the challenge, develop new awareness, and discover hidden skills and aspirations. Of course, no one can eliminate unpredictable events or negative change completely. Health problems, emotional conflict, and other difficult situations arise for us all, and they are unavoidable. But being aware of the shifts in your values, attitudes, skills, and knowledge can minimize much wrenching change in other areas of your life by encouraging a more gradual evolution of skills and self-confidence. This is how you convert the crisis at the crossroads into a successful path forward. As you learn from your experience, you become better prepared to cope with other disruptions that confront you.

Circumstances leading to a juncture that requires a life change can be intensely personal or job-related. In the cases of Kelley Lawrence, Aaron Roberts, and Jennifer Carr, both causes came into play. Sometimes it comes as a bolt of lightning, as in Kelley's case. And sometimes it evolves as an understanding based on accumulated perceptions and evidence, as was the case for Aaron and Jennifer. In all three instances, however, the consequence was the same: It was learning and knowledge informed by their experience that put them in a position to get and hold a different and better job.

▶ Holly Palmer

"It's funny when you look back at your life and what had seemed like a series of random events actually takes on a collective meaning and importance that hadn't been obvious before. And that's what has happened to me as a result of making the decision to go back to college and get my BA.

I started at the University of Minnesota when I was eighteen. It was okay, but I quickly realized that I had always wanted to be in radio. As a result, I dropped out and went to a technical college and got a Certificate in Broadcasting. From university to technical school was a pretty big change. I always thought I'd go back, but eventually I got pregnant and that took care of that.

I was happy in radio. And successful. I got hired immediately and worked for a local broadcaster in the Twin Cities. It went very well. I had a lot of success there. After about ten years, I was recruited to come to the east coast for a job with a big communications company. I said 'yes' and moved to Connecticut.

The time here has been wonderful—a great run during which I have done well and moved up. All without a degree. So what changed the equation? I had a bad experience, a slap in the face, if you will, about five years ago and it changed everything. I was up for a 'woman in technology' award and, lo and behold, I won the award. A real thrill.

Afterwards, I was talking with the woman who made the presentation and she asked me where I got my degree. When I told her I didn't have one, she turned on her heel and walked away without saying a word. Just turned around and walked away. What made it even worse was that she was a woman.

I had migrated to technology from being on the air in radio because I was very good at it. It's a very male enterprise, so as a woman, I was familiar with that uphill battle. But to have a woman react like that shocked me to my core. On the spot, I became determined that would never happen again. I had always thought that I'd go back to college when my son graduated from college. But, after that kick in the teeth, I wasn't going to wait.

Before that moment I had several reasons, justifications if you will, why the timing for college wasn't right for me. I now realize that the barriers I encountered, the things that I used as reasons to not go to college, were of my own construction. Like finances. I needed to focus on my son's needs for college first. I told myself that I wouldn't have time, that it would be too much work and make my life too complicated. But, of course, as I look back at it now, I was afraid of failing. That fear of being unsuccessful underlay all the other reasons.

I immediately started looking for colleges and came across Charter Oak State College in early 2012. I read everything on their website. I didn't understand all the options, but my wonderful advisor helped me understand other ways of getting credit. In the beginning, I decided to just bring in my nineteen transfer credits and take a few courses and see what happened next.

Thanks to my advisor, I eventually used my experience to get credit where I needed it—about fifteen credits. I could have gotten a lot more if I had chosen a degree in the technology area. However, I wanted to use the college experience to learn things that I didn't know. I wanted more than a piece of paper to hang on my wall; I wanted the knowledge that went with it. I decided to learn organizational leadership, moving away from engineering and technology. I think that's a better future for me at work if I want to move up and get new challenges. I used the experiential credit to get the requirements for non-major electives in subjects that I already knew about out of the way, primarily in communications based on my broadcasting experience. When I got to the end of my required classes, I took the assessed credit to hasten the completion. I'll get my BA this fall.

Getting the experiential credit was fascinating, I enjoyed the process. You had to find the class that you are going to challenge. You look for different syllabi and then find the best match. What I totally didn't anticipate was the power that came from being required to write down in detail not only what I learned but also to explore what these experiences meant to me, how they changed me.

Everything fell into place for me, including the realization that my career has been shaped by advice that I got when I was twenty. When I asked my supervisor what I needed to do to be successful, way back in Minnesota at that radio station, he was as emphatic as he was direct. 'Just go for it,' he said. 'Say *yes* when an opportunity arises.' And I realized that although I had put some roadblocks up in my life, I had also gotten them out of the way.

Beyond the credit, however, there was another set of big consequences. As I reviewed my life and the learning I had done, as I reflected on the meaning and consequences of events, I was able to place a value on the people and events that have been helpful. I have been able to see how I feared failure and how I overcame that fear. In line with that, by going for organizational leadership, I am seizing my future. Leadership is where the jobs and the challenges are going to be. I'm going for it. My advisor helped with that.

Another incredible benefit from going back to college later in life was that I got involved with the COSC student association. I got interested in the association and then, after a while, I was elected to the student advisory board to the

Board of Regents. Now I am chair of the statewide student association and a member of the Board of Regents. This has given me a lot more confidence and working with student reps from all seventeen state colleges and universities, about 88,000 students in all, has given me a whole new look at leadership, this time in a policy environment.

What a wonderful opportunity that came from going back to school and being ready to go for it!"

Networking and family relationships have often been the dominant way that people approach decision-making about education and careers. And if it happens that way for you, it's fortunate and likely all for the good. For many of the rest of us, however, getting simple, accurate advice about colleges, training programs, and employment programs or jobs is far more random and hence more difficult and frustrating. Section two will take you through some of those frustrations and share examples of how to overcome them whether they apply to learning or work. Hang on, it's a great ride.

ELIMINATING BARRIERS TO COLLEGE

3

THE SCARECROW'S DILEMMA

SOMETIMES A STORY CAN MAKE the point more clearly than all the explanation in the world. If you find yourself with no way of identifying what you know and no way of giving it value in terms of your personal development, your career, or higher education, remember what happens to the Scarecrow in the 1939 film of *The Wizard of Oz*. Although he exhibited great ingenuity and intelligence throughout his travels with Dorothy, he believed that he knew nothing, that he had "no brain." So he wants to go with Dorothy to ask the Wizard if he can do something about it:

> **Scarecrow**: Do you think if I went with you this Wizard would give me some brains?
>
> **Dorothy**: I couldn't say. But even if he didn't, you'd be no worse off than you are now.
>
> **Scarecrow**: Yes, that's true. . . ."

When they reach Wizard, Scarecrow asks him if he can help him.

Wizard: "Why, anybody can have a brain. That's a very mediocre commodity. Every pusillanimous creature that crawls on the Earth or slinks through slimy seas has a brain. Back where I come from, we have universities, seats of great learning, where people go to become great thinkers. And, when they come out they think deep thoughts, and with no more brains than you have. But they have one thing that you haven't got, a diploma. Therefore, by virtue of the authority vested in me by the Universitatus Committitatum E Pluribus Unum, I hereby confer upon you the Honorary Degree of Th.D—Doctor of Thinkology . . ."

Scarecrow: "Oh!" The sum of the square roots of any two sides of an isosceles triangle is equal to the square root of the remaining side . . . Oh joy! Oh rapture! I've got a brain."[6]

The Scarecrow thought he needed brains. But what he really needed was acknowledgement and recognition that he was a knowledgeable person with skills and learning that were valuable in the eyes of the world and to the people around him. Frank Baum, the author of *The Wizard of Oz*, made light of the Scarecrow's dilemma. But for you, the same dilemma can have serious consequences.

"So near and yet so far." That simple phrase describes the traditional feeling about college for many people. Maybe you have had that experience. The local college is right there, you pass it every day on your way to go shopping or to work. But when it comes to actually attending that college, it feels like it's a million miles away, on another planet. A person I interviewed told me the following story about himself:

"Ed was frustrated and pensive. For the third time in three years, he had been passed over for a job promotion that he knew he could handle. As he left the HR office with the bad news, it finally began to sink in. Even with his learning from the army and a year at the local community college, his college record didn't add up to a degree. And it took a degree to qualify for the position. As he drove home, Ed felt as if he were in a straitjacket, but that it was made of gauze. He could move, but he couldn't go anywhere. He thought angrily, *That college is right down the road from where I work. I drive past it every morning on my way in and every night on my way out. And yet it might as well be a million miles away! That's no 'shining city on a hill.' That's a castle with the drawbridge pulled up. But what else can I do but look into going back to school?*"[7]

If you have felt that way, there are good reasons for that feeling. There are two different sets of obstacles for working adults at the vast majority of colleges. First, your life is already complicated. You may have children and others who depend on you for support. Or, there may be many unstated reasons and fears that hold you back from finding out more and going to college. And there is always the need to work, to earn a living. How can you fit college into that kind of complicated and busy life?

The second set of obstacles is personal in another way. You don't know where to begin. And, equally as important, you sense that college wasn't designed with you, or the life you are living, in mind. Where is the advice to help you think through courses and goals? Where is the financial support to temper the risk of accumulating debt as you proceed? Where are the other support services that respect the realities that you bring with you the same way that colleges cater to eighteen-year-olds just out of high school? Do you really want to pay for a climbing wall and boutiques? Instead, how about childcare and convenient parking?

As you will see in chapters 4 and 5, there are "adult-friendly" colleges that will help you take control over your personal learning and hidden credentials and surround you with other "adult-friendly" services. But first it is important to understand the unseen obstacles that hold so many people back from the learning and work that they want.

When Gulliver was restrained by the Lilliputians, he knew what the problem was. He was tied down. But for many frustrated learners, their bonds are invisible. In some cases, those bonds are self-imposed. In still other cases, they are imposed by a traditional set of policies and practices which were formulated for recent high school graduates, not you.

Over the past several years, I have written a blog (www.rethinkinghighereducation.net) about this issue and other problems that beset higher education in America. Several years ago, a woman named "Faith" wrote me the following post after reading one such blog.

> "I am an experienced older American worker. I have gained streams of workplace experience that were obtained without a formal education . . . (My life) situation forced me to take this path. Now, to get the same job that I've held for so many years, I need a degree. I can't change my past, but what about me now? I shouldn't be ruled out. People like myself hold wells of workplace experience that are still useful and productive and can help with this employment situation."[8]

Faith is just one of the millions of people who have been left in the dust by traditional education's approach which says, "Classroom first, and nothing else matters." Each person's case, taken individually, may seem like a sad song; perhaps even a little whiney. But millions of such cases, taken together, create a rising chorus of pain and waste which crescendos into a weaker social and civic life and a declining ability to compete in the global economy.

Why is this important? Let me share, briefly, my philosophy on this point. America and the American promise stand at the intersection of two powerful concepts and life forces: liberty and justice. Liberty is the icon of individualism, the inalienable right of the individual to life, liberty, and the pursuit of happiness. It promises that we will be free from the domination of others, free to speak, to practice religion—or not, as we please—to make our own ways in the world.

But liberty is balanced out by justice, a competing and comple-mentary concept. Justice speaks to the common good, the commit-ment that all people will be treated fairly under the law. We agree that there are legitimate interests of the many over the few, to be moderated and determined by the three branches of government.

Some would argue that America's greatness is captured in our institutions of government, the Bill of Rights, the Constitution, and the separation of powers among the three branches of govern-ment. As revolutionary and historic as these documents and con-cepts are, however, they are only the skin and bones of democracy. They would mean little without a citizenry willing to believe in them. I believe that the genius in American democracy lies in hope, the promise of opportunity for all, a belief that your chil-dren will have a better life than you.

The presence of hope in people's hearts is what makes America great and binds our society together, carrying oxygen to all parts of our civic and social body. If the promise of opportunity is the bloodstream of America, then learning and education are the mighty beating heart that makes the blood flow, creating and nur-turing our human talent.

The American promise says that there will be as many seats at the table of opportunity as there are people who wish to take one. In America, you do not have to wait for someone to die or push someone off their seat to get your opportunity. Here, we say that you don't have to stand in line. If you work hard, you can grab the dream and have a seat at the table of opportunity with everyone else.[9]

Compare that promise with Alan's experience. Like Faith, Alan, another respondent to my blog, addressed the consequences of not having access to a degree:

"I am one of the two-thirds of Americans without the degree that you mentioned. I have been running my own business for the last ten years. During that time, I have acquired nu-merous skills and a tremendous amount of knowledge. I am now at a point in my life where I want to move on to the next challenge. Unfortunately, any job listing I come across that I am qualified for in regards to the position, I do not meet the educational requirements.

I know in my heart that I have plenty to offer. I also know that a degree will open more doors for me. I have looked into getting credit for my work experience, but even that process is cumbersome and remote for a working adult with a family. The kind of aggressive innovation that adults like me need involves streamlining that process. Instead of discouraging people like me, embrace us and discover the talent and innovation we can bring to the workforce."

Looking at the traditional model of higher education, we can see several different components of a "success ceiling" that conspire to keep adults out.

- Colleges are psychologically remote, holding people away with a reputation as places that are alien to the needs of working adults. They have the aura and mystery of the unknown, or forbidden fruit. And you, the learner, may have been convinced that you are a "loser."
- Colleges are, generally, experientially remote. They don't recognize the value of learning that happens somewhere else, outside of college. Imagine having your entire life experience—work, personal, and social—nullified by an arbitrary historic practice.
- Colleges are physically remote, requiring a time, and time of week, commitment that simply does not align well with other demands on an adult's life. Colleges are academically remote, refusing to honor credits earned at other colleges, in the military, or in corporate training. Colleges are financially remote, requiring too much expense and debt for many working adults to get to the degree.

- Most colleges have enrollment limits, enforced by funding, space, and reputation, making them unavailable to many people.[9]

To the person on the outside looking in, any one of these obstacles may be huge. But when taken in combination, they appear to be evidence that college is for someone else. Millions of good people simply do not have an option. They are defeated by "the way things have always been."

Too often, colleges' daily practices act as roadblocks for adult learners. Some examples are:

- The computer requirements are unclear and getting appropriate support is difficult.
- You have a job and your academic advisor doesn't have evening hours, and the courses you need are scheduled when you can't attend.
- There is no access to daycare, and parking is remote and scarce.
- There is no recognition of your personal learning.[10]

For many adults, however, maybe even for you, the sheer complexities and realities of life intervening becomes the obstacle that is overwhelming. You will meet up with Linda West, Irving Gomez, and Andrew Hogan again later on in the book. But their early life stories illustrate just how easy it is to get offtrack when it comes to college.

▶ Linda West

"I am a lifelong learner. I have always loved books, I owe this completely to my mother; she signed me up for a new program, Reading Is Fundamental (RIF). I was seven years old. At that time we lived in the inner city of Hartford. We had a large family—mom, dad, and five children—and we had to share everything! The books from RIF were the only thing that I really owned. I cherished them. I loved going up the ramp into that truck with its library. It was like a little special heaven.

From that point on, I wanted everything that the books had. I am self-taught. If I want to learn something, my first move is to get a book on the topic. I keep a journal, and take notes to remember. At one point in my life, I did about eighteen months of Spanish, watching Spanish television, studied Spanish books, and listened to audio lessons. Besides the language itself, I learned there was a big difference among Spanish dialects.

You might ask me, 'What happened about college?' When I graduated from high school, I wanted to go to college but I had no clue how to do that. I was from a blue-collar African-American family. My parents both worked in factories and eventually moved us to the suburbs. But I was never able to afford to go to college when I was young. My parents did not attend school beyond eighth grade. Theirs was a very different experience growing up during the fifties in the south.

This meant if I was going to go to college, I was on my own. In high school, girls were getting pregnant and moving in with their boyfriends. I decided I would never do that. I saw the movie *Private Benjamin*, and I (along with thousands of other young women), joined the Army and served for almost 6 years. I loved the discipline, and I accumulated a lot of money for college through the GI bill. But after I left the army, life intervened. I got married and had kids. I got sidetracked.

Don't get me wrong. I loved being a Mom. I gave my life to my children, two boys and two girls. My husband and I were happy for a while, and then not so much. After my divorce, I did not return to work until my youngest was in 1st grade. I was available for field trips with them. We traveled, went to parks. Everything.

My first tries at college were a disaster. I had no advice, no coach. So, I blew my GI Bill money on a series of "approved" rip-off trade schools that eventually went out of business. I got a poor education and there was little or no record of what I had done.

What triggered my decision to go back this time was an incident at work. One day, I overheard a manager discussing me and my future and she said, about me, 'She doesn't have a BA.' And I was torn up!

I felt terrible for a couple of weeks. But then I said, 'Linda, it's your fault. How many times did you start out for college and then stop? It's your responsibility to do something about this situation!' The reality was that they were paying me $52K a year to do filing. So now in addition to being upset and focused, I realized for the first time that I had the time and the energy, the room in my life, to go to school. I was committed, but I had a lot of failure behind me.

A little earlier, my daughter got pregnant with her second child and I asked her to move in with me. She was a student at Kaplan University and she had live professors in real classrooms online. I was listening to her go to school sitting at the dining room table, and I was loving it! It was her last year at Kaplan, and we went to her graduation in Chicago in June 2014 where she graduated with a BS in Business.

As she was finishing, I was just starting. When I returned to school at forty-nine, it was the first time that I had done something purely for myself. Now it was my turn. That experience at work and watching my daughter do her thing were what drove me back to college, for real, this time.

My self-esteem and confidence went through the roof. I never questioned my aptitude or my ability. But it was hard work, working, going to school, juggling my grandchildren and their play when my daughter worked on weekends. It was hard to get the work done. But it was also a strong confirmation of my intelligence and what I had learned over all those years. Many of the classes confirmed my life experience.

At work, my mental state changed as well. I had to confront my fears and try to understand what was happening. Listen to positive motivations, do self-talks and confront that fear. I came to realize that the person who I had been for all those years had changed dramatically."

Linda was on her own. Doing the best that she could. Clearly intelligent and reflective, she had nowhere to turn for the advice that she needed that might connect her to programs that would meet her needs and life circumstances. And then the lights went on, thanks to her experience at work and her daughter's example. Finding the right college made all the difference.

▶ Irving Gomez

Irving Gomez, however, was an entirely different kettle of fish. In his own words, Irving knew "that I was supposed to go to college." But it took years for him to get an answer to the questions that mattered, "What do I want to be when I grow up?" and "How can college help me get where I want to go personally and professionally?" Hear Irving describe the many years that he simply bounced around from school to school and job to job, with no one but friends to give him occasional advice.

"When I graduated from high school in 1996, I didn't have a plan or a clue about what I wanted to do personally or professionally. But I knew I was supposed to go to college, so I beat on that door for quite a while, with very little success. First, I tried Florida State because I loved football and sports, and they were big in those areas—But they turned me down.

I then applied to John Jay College of Criminal Justice which was local to me, and I thought my interest in criminal investigations might produce a focus in criminology. As I learned more and studied the field of criminology, I realized it was not what I wanted to pursue. And my grades suffered, so much so that I flunked out of John Jay.

On their advice I went to Kingsborough Community College in Brooklyn to raise my grades. I was telling myself that I went there to get my grades up and go back to John Jay. I actually did get my associate's degree in TV and radio broadcasting, but I wasn't going to go back to John Jay. I was still just floating with no plan, looking for a degree without a defined purpose. While trying to build a semblance of a pIan, I went to Brooklyn College where I started to work on a sports broadcasting bachelor's degree. But that didn't work for me either, and after a while I flunked out of Brooklyn College.

Through all this I managed to secure a two-month internship at NFL Films in New Jersey. I literally begged the facilitator to take a shot on me. NFL Films is the homegrown media company of the National Football League, whose work is respected and appreciated by many fans of the NFL. I did not live in New Jersey (where NFL Films is) and did not drive. So, the crazy commute from New York City to the internship in Mt. Laurel, New Jersey, underscored my true interest to pursue sports.

I did my best and put my heart into the work. At the end of the internship I was offered a job. I said 'yes' before I found out my expected pay. When I was informed that it was to be eight dollars an hour, I was crushed. It was not that I simply wanted more money. I just couldn't afford it. The combination of moving to a new apartment in another state with no car on such little pay appeared to set me up for a dire situation. Since they were not willing to budge I had to give a painstaking "no" and not take the job.

For the next few years, I did a bunch of jobs in different offices. I was freelancing and failed to improve my grades in school. Nothing special. And I thought it was over. This was the life I had. The lowest point for me professionally was when I ended doing a security job at a small Verizon store in Manhattan. I was literally walking people from the entrance of the store to the booth to service their phones. Back and forth all day, every day. I had given up on any professional goals at that point."

Still another learner, Andrew Hogan, found that the traditional college academic structure foiled him time and again. He knew "what" to do. But the traditional structure wouldn't adapt to his learning and behavioral needs. See how, despite being put on the "outside looking in," Andrew's natural intelligence and resourcefulness kept him in the game of life.

▶ Andrew Hogan

"I have had a pretty unusual path through life up to this day. It was not the case that I couldn't get into a college. I graduated from a very good day school in Greenwich, Connecticut, and actually tried college a number of times. The big issue was that I couldn't stay in college. I had a terrible time with tests, the pressure of the clock on the wall and finishing on time. And the classroom conversations were hell for me. I just didn't feel comfortable participating and competing.

When I first graduated from high school, I went to Hampshire College. I tried biology and fine arts, but the environment just did me in. So I finally decided to 'do' my art, in this case photography, leave college, and travel. A few years later, I tried again, and went to the Boston School of Fine Arts. And it was wonderful. But again I just couldn't stand the classroom environment. I decided to leave and did more travel and worked odd jobs to make ends meet.

Then I got married, and we decided that I'd give it one more try, this time at NYU. But I failed again because the classroom setting and testing, the whole way it was set up, drove me crazy. It just wasn't for me. So strike three and you are out. I left again.

Then I came to phase two. My wife had a goal and a focus, and I wanted to do art. She was going gangbusters at Yale, working through a PhD, and then Law School and writing a book. I decided to put a lot of things on the shelf, and when she had our kids, I became a stay-at-home Dad. Caring for them and doing my art.

During all of that time, I kept working on photography, traveling and at home, but delaying, driven by fear, presenting to galleries or doing a show or applying to school. That's the truth of it. I was very, very scared of school or any other situation where I might be publicly accountable. But I kept doing my projects and saving the material that I shot.

As the kids got older, just starting high school, my time became freer, I became somewhat horrified that I no longer had the "job" of parenting because that began to reopen the prospect of school and taking charge of my own professional life. I started looking at graduate schools, but put it all off again. Too much fear. But then, as the kids moved through college (he laughs sheepishly), I felt some financial pressure and also thought that it was time to get a degree.

I had separated from my wife, though we are still good friends. And I married again, this time to a terrific woman who is an MD. I felt it was time to 'carry my own weight' a little more. And I had been thinking about teaching high school or college as a perfect solution to having a balance between making art and teaching it. I had taught in high schools and other settings over the previous ten years—part-time, but paid. And I really enjoyed it.

I started looking for teaching positions, and guess what? I found that in order to teach at almost any level you need a master's degree. And if you want to teach in high school, you absolutely need a BA or BFA. Now, maybe if I had had exhibitions in the National Gallery of the Metropolitan Museum of Art, they'd make an exception. But I had not. So I hit another road block: as I entered my fifties, if I wanted to teach, I needed a BA because you need one to even begin to qualify for a master's.

But there were two big problems facing me in this pursuit. First, I was still terrified of the academic life after what I had experienced in high school and my three college tries. Behaviorally, I am a quiet person, and the classroom also terrifies me. And the pressure around testing is unbearable. It's not that I don't know the stuff. But I freeze.

Second was another complication. I needed the degree, but I couldn't just leave home for a traditional program with a traditional schedule and time commitment. I couldn't just up and go off to school the way I had three times before. I was high and dry again."

If any of these stories ring true to you, that's because they reflect an unspoken reality. Despite expending tremendous effort, time, and money to improve services to adult learners, most American colleges are not organized to be suitable for people like Linda, Irving, and Andrew. These are people who did not fit the traditional student stereotype. They needed accommodation in multiple and different ways. Better information and advising, better accessibility, improved financial advice, and an academic program that could adapt to their learning strengths, among other things.

Importantly, also, the mythology that surrounds colleges even today favors learners who come from a college tradition or are at least "the right age." Part of this disconnect is the fact that most colleges still do not value your hidden credentials as an asset that is worth academic recognition. As a result, your work or artistic history is not respected and you can't get "advanced placement" which aligns your knowledge with appropriate courses in the curriculum. So you lose.

This is exacerbated by the emotional alienation that many people feel from higher education. They believe that college is not meant for them—that they don't belong there. Maybe you have felt that way as well. These self-inflicted feelings are not wrong. In many cases they reflect accurately the history of people who have been excluded from the colleges near them.

To compound the problem, most employers, despite protesting to the contrary, still rely on traditional credentials to make hiring decisions. At the same time, they criticize the readiness of recent college graduates to work. In real time, the gap between working adults and college is reflected by a similar gap between them and work.

▶ Peg Moore

Peg told me her story many years ago. And it still rings true as she discusses the continuing problems and uncertainties she faced because she didn't have a degree.

"When I had my third child, I was still working at home. I became very interested in the health care of the community because two of my children were asthmatics. I found it extremely difficult to get help here for them. One day, I heard there was a meeting in the community around health care issues, so I went to it and began to go to these meetings regularly. Eventually, the group asked me to chair the meetings. I knew absolutely nothing about chairing a meeting. I didn't know protocol, and I still don't. But I did it.

After working just over a year, we were able to open the doors of this health care facility and begin providing services to the community. They were very much needed and very much used.

Then, the board asked me to take on the job as director of the center. I was very uncomfortable with that because I was concerned that I wouldn't do the community just service because I had no education. But I knew what the community would accept and what they would not. I also knew my limitations and I wasn't afraid to ask for help.

So, reluctantly, I decided to take on the role with the help of some friends in the health care field. They said they would tell me to get out if I wasn't doing a just service to the community by holding this job without a degree . . . if that was a hindrance to the center.

I've changed a lot over the years since I got involved. When I began— when I tell people this they laugh because they know me now—I was shy, very unsure of myself, and lacking any self-confidence. Yet, to this day, I can't tell you why. Actually, I think I changed around the time that I took this job. I used to be very much in awe of people. If someone was a doctor or a lawyer or a teacher, it was like, 'Oh, my god, they're better than I am.' There are a lot of people who are like me when it comes to dealing with professional people.

Working in this job, I found out that everyone is a human being. You put your pants on the same way I do. I had to stop being in awe of people and begin to feel as if I was on the same level so that I could be successful at what I was trying to do. As a result, among other things, my negotiating skills with folks like them became much stronger.

It's a matter of putting myself in a position where I feel as if I'm dealing with someone as an equal. Early on in the game, they were calling me 'Peg' and I was calling them 'Doctor.' Then I got to the point where I said, 'Well, I love a first name basis so you call me Peg and I'll call you Peter.' That put us on equal terms when we were talking. When we're in the examining room, that's another situation because you're the professional and I'm the client. But at the table, that's a different deal.

There was something else I learned that was really important. I used to sit in meetings, listening to someone speak. And I would get into a panic because I didn't know what in god's name they were talking about. I would think, 'What am I doing here? I'm out of my element, it's beyond me, it's over my head!' It affected me so much that sometimes I thought I was going to cry or pass out or both. I wasn't understanding a damn word that was being said.

I would look around and everybody was like engrossed in the conversation, nodding, the whole bit. Well, finally something gave me the courage at one meeting to say, 'Excuse me, I don't know if there is something wrong with me, but I don't understand what you just said.' Ninety percent of the people in the room said, 'You're right, I don't understand it either.' We were all too embarrassed to admit we didn't understand what the hell the guy was talking about because we didn't want to sound stupid."

We see that Peg has developed more confidence, self-awareness, and skills since she took the job at the health center. And she has become more assertive, adept in the rules and group dynamics as well. Peg became a competent health care service manager on the job and became extremely knowledgeable about the services her center offered as well as its financial condition. As she said, ". . . I know that I learn something every day. I know that I've learned something when I can take it and apply it to something else. Then I've learned it."

Still, however, Peg worried about her lack of a degree.

"The sad part is that the degree—that piece of paper—is very meaningful to other people. It was really frowned on when I would send a proposal into a government agency and they would ask what my background was. I graduated from high school. Period. I mean it was like, 'What? You don't have a master's degree?' They were thinking, 'What do you have, a Mickey Mouse operation going on there?'

You just can't seem to get your foot inside the door without the degree. I know a man who works in an insurance company. He has all kinds of certificates from school programs and conferences and things he's done in the insurance business. But when an opening occurred elsewhere in the building, he applied and they said, 'Well, you don't have the degree.' (Her voice dripping with sarcasm) They would take someone with a degree in gardening because they had the piece of paper and bypass the person who has the experience in the area where they are looking. It happens all the time. It is very frustrating!"

Peg got her job by coincidence, with some luck and good circumstances. But as the world and her job changed around her, she felt the rub between her talent and knowledge on the one hand and the need for a formal credential on the other.

The Scare Crow's dilemma is alive and well for millions of adult learners. They have been busy traveling down the road of life, gaining knowledge through lived experience, yet held at arm's length away from the opportunities that validation of their hidden credentials would bring. That's the situation that is being changed as we speak by adult-friendly colleges that are organized with you, the learner, in mind.

4

ADULT-FRIENDLY COLLEGES

HELP IS ON THE WAY for Scarecrow, Peg Moore, and all the other people trapped in the college gap.

There are some colleges that make you feel welcomed, supported, and "at home" whether you attend a campus or learning center or you are learning online. This chapter will make the case for assessing your hidden credentials. And it will also tell the stories of learners who found an adult-friendly college with a wide array of adult-friendly services that met their needs. And the next chapter will describe, in the words of five presidents, what you have a right to expect, as an adult learner, from colleges going forward.

I learned the importance of assessing personal learning up close and personal back in 1970 when I was just beginning to plan the Community College of Vermont. I was meeting with a group of child care workers and head start mothers in the Northeast Kingdom of Vermont. At the time, the "Kingdom," as it was known, was a remote part of a very rural state. Most people there had no access to college, and if you were an adult, you were out of luck. Period.

These people were excited about a college that would come to where they lived and meet their learning needs. This was our mantra. And I had just finished describing a new kind of a college for poor and working Vermonters designed especially to bring education to them in places and at times that were convenient. I had explained carefully that, because of this need for flexibility and responsiveness, we would not be tied to tradition. There would be no credits or degrees, just courses that interested them, like child development. I was taking a page from Ivan Illich's book, *Deschooling Society*, and I was feeling very progressive.

But one of the women there, Margery Hood, wasn't buying it. There was anger in the air—averted eyes, heavy silence, shifting chairs.

"You! With your college degree on the wall, are telling us we don't need one?" Her face flushed and her voice rising, Margery continued. "What do you think we are, dumb? We *need* credit. If you're not going to be tied to college traditions, you should start by giving credit for the things we have already learned working here."

Margery needed help all right. But not the help I was offering. She was trapped by a reality I had ignored. Everything she knew she had learned raising her family on a Vermont farm and working at the child care center. She was very good at her work. But colleges and other employers did not recognize or accept that kind of learning when she looked for another job or tried to further her education.[11]

As I drove home that night, I questioned myself.

- Should childcare workers with years of experience on the job as well as job-related training be treated like 18-year-old freshmen by the college?
- No.
- Did it make good educational sense to recognize and reward learning that had happened away from school and give credit for that learning as well as other coursework offered?

- Yes. If we did it well.
- Should an employer look beyond paper credentials to a person's actual experience, behavior, and ability when assessing their capacity and potential to perform?
- Yes, if they wanted to get the best that each person had to offer and achieve a good "fit" between the person and the workplace.[12]

And so we decided that we would meet Margery's challenge and give academic recognition for prior learning in an outcome-based curriculum. I believe that this single decision was *the* turning point in the academic development of the college during its early years.

Assessing your learning, wherever and however it was accomplished, has enormous payoff in academic and career value. And as you have read already, it also has tremendous personal impact for the person doing it. After almost fifty years of experience, I believe that it is the cornerstone of successful learning throughout life for many adults. You will see, in the examples and stories which follow, how assessment will connect your hidden credentials with college and career in a triangle of opportunity.

▶ Peg Moore

Peg Moore, extraordinarily successful as the founding administrator of a health care center in Boston's North End, knew that her lack of a degree raised questions in the minds of professional and funding agencies during the early days of her tenure. The questions always seemed to connect her lack of formal preparation with the credibility of the program, even though all available evidence pointed to success.

Eventually, Peg decided to get her degree. Her decision was a classic blend of practicality and personal learning. Peg needed the "piece of paper." But she acted upon her decision to go back to school only when she found a college that was friendly to her situation.

"I didn't know what the future was going to bring, and I saw this as an opportunity to do something about it for myself. It was tremendously exciting. But it was very difficult to hold down a full-time job, go to school, take care of my family, and do it all in fifteen months. I literally dragged myself to school and just about cried in the classroom to get through it.

I see so many people coming out of school with a degree in their hand and, quite frankly, they don't know what to do with it. They've learned in the books, but it's not the real world. The book learning is only a base and kids coming out of college don't know what to do with it.

The actual deciding factor in my going was that I learned about a program that allowed me to use some of the things that I had already accomplished toward the degree, so it wouldn't take that long. Therefore, I wouldn't have to go the formal four-year program route with four courses a semester to achieve the degree. I didn't have the time, the inclination or the patience to do that.

I think the important component of this whole thing is that if you have a degree and no common sense (and there's nothing in any school that I know of that teaches you that) then you really do have a worthless piece of paper. I think some of it has to come from either personal experience— the real world experience, in some business or other venture, be it when you were younger or whatever, and then apply that to an education, then you've got a good combination.

Colleges need to change also. I'd want courses that were going to be related to real-world situations. They need to be taught by people who have done it; not only by educators.

The point is, whether you learn on the job or on the street or in the classroom, if you have the talent and the common sense, you can do it. You can apply it. You can make it work. Take my case. I knew the community, and I cared about what happened to the community and the people in it. You can't learn that part very easily. It takes a long time, and you really have to want to learn it. The other part, the health care administrative academic part can be learned quicker and faster.

I can't imagine going to a marriage counselor who isn't married and has no children who asks, 'Are you having trouble with your children?' and then tries to give you advice on how to deal with them. They haven't gone through it. So, in most cases, their advice is going to be limited. I'm sure a few could do it. But, how could you possibly imagine what it's like to live with a teenager?"

Peg was lucky. She found an "adult-friendly" college which, for all its faults, understood about the importance of her personal learning and incorporated her experience factor into her advanced standing in the program. An adult-friendly college knows that, for you, an education is only one part of a complicated and busy life. It is accessible to you personally as well as being responsive to your needs and life situation.

▶ Jason DeForge

Jason DeForge was in a rut at work. He had missed out on college and then life's responsibilities caught up with him. But twenty years later, he had an opportunity to take another crack at college, beginning with a reflection on his experiential and job-based learning over the years and their value to him going forward. Listen to Jason as he came to understand the depth and impact of his learning, and how it changed his life.

"I left college twice, once because I wasn't ready, and once because of a family emergency. So college went on the back burner for years. In fact, I stopped even thinking about it as a possibility. I had kids and responsibilities. It was live and work, no college.

I got a job, went to work, and began to move up. I took every training I could get. And I even started leading some training. One day, my supervisor noticed me leading a training session and, as she said later, she thought she saw a spark in me. She approached me and urged me to return to college, beginning with a course that assessed my prior experiential learning at CCV.

I was totally divorced from any knowledge of my personal learning. Had no idea what was in there. But as I got going, I saw my life rolling out in front of me. It was incredible. I met with professionals who gave me oral exams and then made a judgment. And I received other documentation from people with whom I had worked. It was **very** positive because it was a tremendous affirmation for me and the valuing of all this experience that I had completely forgotten.

One of the things that I had to do was write an essay that told my story from high school to that point in time—twenty years. I was astonished at how much I had forgotten about what I had done and what it meant to me. I had forgotten so much of what I had done and learned. I loved the experience, and it changed my life.

Sure, getting advanced standing with assessed prior learning saved me time and money. That was important. But the unanticipated, additional gift was something very powerful mentally and emotionally. When I first dove into it, I was afraid there would be no "there, there," that I wouldn't have enough learning to justify doing the course.

But I was selling myself short and ignoring important parts of my life and experience. Like I had worked at a print shop, and I discovered that the learning I did there was equal to some early college-level computer courses. The big difference was this. When you learn something for the first time in college, it is an abstraction without real world context. But when you learn it at work, it is real time with added dimension, value and meaning because it is in a real-world context.

This has been a life-changing experience for me."

You met Kelley Lawrence briefly in chapter 2. But her comments below on the impact of coming to reflect on and understand her personal learning hits the bull's-eye. She said,

> "It (the assessment course) changed my life. It taught me to love learning, and it opened my eyes to what I had actually learned since high school. I was shocked, but equally astounded and pleased. As I got to thinking about all that I had done, the looking back and placing a value on things helped me see a new direction. Those eleven years had great value to me that I had never noticed. As I got a grasp on what I had learned, it was like a whole new world opened up. And I was able to focus more on my passions, the things I loved to do."

And Irving Gomez, trapped in a dead-end job, finally got the break, and the break-through, that he needed at an adult-friendly college.

> "I moved to Connecticut (where my friend had also moved to work at the company where I got the job) and lived with my friend. He was like a brother and helped me navigate through the waters of change and growth. This was a great company and a great job! I was really happy there. I had always loved sports so it seemed like a great match. Things were looking up.
>
> After a couple years, however, I was passed up for a promotion because I didn't have the BA. I was first offered the job, and then the HR office realized I did not have my bachelor's degree. Because of certain "rules" they needed me to have that first. This disappointment Ied me to return to school again to spruce up my resume. The school was Tunxis Community College. Well, this time I did well in the courses I liked, but without focus and no follow-through the time remaining in school seemed insurmountable to me, and I stopped attending yet again.

Then, about two years later, another friend told me about Charter Oak State College, and he continually argued that I should attend. He also had many credits but no bachelors, and then he had gone to Charter Oak State College. He obtained his bachelor's degree a lot faster than he originally thought he would. His appreciation of his experience led him to push me to do the same.

As I look back on that period of time, I did not understand that in wasting my time I was also wasting a valuable commodity. You don't get time back. And I wasn't asking, 'how can college help me get where I want to go personally and professionally?' I was just going through the motions of what I thought I was supposed to be doing.

So I considered Charter Oak one more time. I spoke with a counselor named Jennifer, and, with her advice and help, I took a totally different direction. I decided to major in history. I have always loved history and done well in history courses. But I had never before actually connected with the love I had for it. Now I am focused on a career in history later in life. I officially enrolled in a general studies degree with a concentration in history. I hope to graduate in December. I want to work in history—whether a school or a museum—so I am pursuing the BA and then a master's degree in public history. Then I will examine what are the opportunities available.

Charter Oak made all the difference. I got incredible counseling and support from my counselor, Jennifer. She is very encouraging to me, regularly offering advice relevant to my goals.

My goal is to get my bachelors fast and save time and money. But that has meant taking some tests and getting recognition for previous experiential learning for advanced standing. Jennifer recommended I take tests for credit instead of classes, but I am a terrible test-taker so I ducked and took the standard class at first. But the class was too expensive and lasted too long for me. I was teetering on quitting once more, caught between not going fast enough and my fear of testing.

But Jennifer stayed after me, telling me to just buckle down, get the help I needed, and take the tests. So I did. Since 2015 I have passed five tests and have two remaining. In the end, I will have saved over $6,000 dollars. It was a great feeling to know that this avenue existed. It respected my circumstances, and once I got over my doubt, it saved me time and money by giving value for what I already knew. Every time I pass a test, I celebrate. I am so grateful for the opportunity and my advisor who gave me the guts to do something that I didn't see and didn't want to do. I needed that kick in the pants. It helped me think differently about what I wanted to do with my life.

Along the way, my aspirations have changed as well. I love my current job. I love the place. However, I have stopped striving to get the "dream job" there. The more I've looked at it, the more I have seen that the people who hold the positions that I thought I wanted were not happy personally. I did not want the 'dream job' at the expense of my marriage or peace of mind. I didn't want to fall in love with the desire for more money in my career and life. Now I'm on a different path. Although I appreciate my job and will work as best as I can for the time being, it is not my path to happiness any longer.

I chose a different future over stagnation at work. Ultimately I want more control over my life. I want to be doing something that is more intellectually rewarding and that brings a better balance between my work and personal life. And that feels great."

▶ Marie Padilla

"The early stages of my life after high school have a lot of common ingredients with other life stories I have heard. I went to the University of Rhode Island for a semester but didn't like it. I thought I was going to be a travel agent. But I moved to California, got a retail job and moved up quickly. Then I got married, had a kid and moved back to RI. It's all kind of a blur—those first few years after high school. I was plenty smart, but I wasn't getting any traction.

Then came step one along the path to where I am today. I got badly hurt in an accident, and I was no longer able to stand up all day. That took care of the retail work. So I bit the bullet and went to the community college, got an associate degree, and became a health-care case manager at a hospital.

That worked for a while because I was raising my girls, and that took time and effort as well. As they graduated high school and went to college, however, I had to face the college thing again. I was stuck with no BA. But that's what I needed to get ahead. I checked out local colleges but found none of them would honor the degree that I had received. They wanted me to start all over again, four more years! That was as expensive as it was insulting. There was no way I was going to go that route.

I just needed to get it done asap. I was in a box and wanted to get out. In my position I couldn't move up. I'd been told that so many times. And then I heard about a college that would assess all my prior learning and give me advanced standing with it. It was funny. I had been in a leadership position many times. So I took the leadership course syllabus and recreated the information from my work in that format. I did that again and again with many courses and it was really cool. I loved the fact that they did it. And I don't understand why more colleges don't do it.

When I went back, though, it was tough. It had been twenty years since the community college, and I was rusty. My first course, called Cornerstones, was awful. I got an 'F' in it and I thought, *I'm done, out the door.* But my advisor just wouldn't let me go. She told me to talk to the teacher and to keep at it.

Of course, because it was online, I could manage my time the way that suited me. Gradually, over time, I got an A- in Cornerstones. And I Iearned to write better and to think more critically as well.

After that it was all A's. But I needed that moral support and the great advice from my advisor and the professors to get past that first hurdle. Professors were giving me feedback, and it was really helpful.

Also, there was a terrific community of students. You create these friendships with people, you get their support and establish relationships outside of class. We had study groups as well. It was hard work, studying and writing, but I made it with everyone's support. You have your own little community.

When I was about halfway through Charter Oak, I heard about a position that had opened up. I applied and got the job even though I hadn't finished the BA at that point. Just being successful in the program was enough to get me the nod.

If I hadn't portfolioed the classes, I wouldn't have graduated in time. So it saved me time and money and got me a job.

I got the job, a 12$ per hour increase. Now I am looking at a master's of science in human services with emphasis in management and leadership. I am just putting the paperwork together. But this will put me in line for even more job improvement.

I am very proud of my daughters. The oldest is in Boston, working for a pharma company. My youngest is looking for work in Boston like biology, and she has an EMT and is doing that on the side. But she is also looking into getting a master's degree in London. So their horizons are huge.

But I am also very proud of what I have done, working fulltime, school fulltime, and taking care of my mother who has Alzheimer's. It's been a busy time with lots of possible pitfalls. But I made it."

► *Keith Waterhouse*

"My life, when it comes to getting a college education, has been a story of years of not caring followed by a burst of activity more recently. When I look back at it, the abrupt change in my attitude about needing and wanting a degree was, ironically, triggered by my success at work. That may sound backwards and upside down, but my success at work actually drove me to get a BS in Organizational Leadership.

My parents didn't push me in high school; nor did they suggest that college was an important option. When I graduated from high school, my Dad said, 'You better get a job. So I did. And I held several jobs over the next five to seven years. Just bouncing around, waiting for something to happen. And then it did. I am going on eighteen years, since I was the age of twenty-five, at my current company.

Here's the ironic part. For the first fifteen years at the company, I was in field services and most of my colleagues didn't have degrees either. So, I never even thought about getting a degree. It was no big deal. I'm doing well, earning good money and working hard every day. Then a job opened up in project management, a higher-level position in the company. So I applied and got the job. Field services was in the rearview mirror.

But there was a big difference in this new job. One that I had never anticipated. Everyone around me, everyone I worked with, inside and outside of the company, had degrees. Although I had a flourishing career, as I looked around, I found that any other work setting would require a degree. I was doing project management without a degree.

This was a deeply personal decision for me. I loved my job and didn't want another one. But not having a degree affected me personally. It felt like it was a stigma. Here I am in a meeting, time after time, when they are taking my word for things, but they have a degree and I do not. I felt small and didn't want to keep feeling that way.

But I also felt vulnerable professionally. Although things were fine at the time in my own small world, I realized that if I stepped outside that world, I would hit a wall. To put it plainly, I wanted to be protected from the vicissitudes that can happen at work. And I knew that having the degree would give me huge confidence. And it has. I stand taller and admire the guy I see in the mirror every morning. To say it plainly, my life today is very different because my self-appraisal is so different because of the work I did to get my degree, and the experiences that I have had.

So once I saw the situation, I wanted to align myself with my peers and I acted fast. I went from not thinking there was a problem to seeing it and doing something about it in about a year. It was pure self-efficacy on my part. It took me about two and a half years to get the four-year BS. I started with 18 credits and CLEP testing got me even farther. Ultimately I got advanced standing for 40 credits and took 80 in place. And I am already enrolled in a master's program at another university.

A lot of my general education credits were filled through assessment of my life experience. Organizational Leadership was the program. They were teaching the theory, and my life experience already had substantiated the theory. So it gave me a context within which to understand more deeply the value of my experience.

For example, on many occasions, even in the online courses, I could tell when other students had not had my experience because they were younger and the theory being taught had not been substantiated by their experience. I could tell that from the way they wrote and the questions they asked. It had a profound impact on me because it underscored the value of what I had learned from my work experience. Now I can publish articles in magazines like *WaterWorld* where I recently published an article on "polyethylene encasement." I've also had articles published on project management and college credit for experience in OpFlow magazine and InFlowLine magazine, respectively.

One of the other drivers for me to go back was the online program. Actually getting to a college physically would have been a huge obstacle for me. I mean I have a job and a family and a life. Being able to go online, coupled with the advanced standing I got through assessment, made all the difference. They saved me time, money, and inconvenience.

When I look back on it, this was not a moment in time kind of a thing, just a thing to do. It has become the basis for a whole new understanding of my life and my future that is grounded in a new understanding of myself. The journey is not over."

You are hearing two important things from Peg, Jason, Keith, and the others. The first is that finding a college that will honor your experience and counsel you as an adult is critical. And the second is that they all reaffirm the power of coming to terms with and understanding your personal learning. In their cases, to repeat my earlier comment, assessment of their prior learning "connected their hidden credentials with college and career in a triangle of opportunity."

5

ADULT-FRIENDLY COLLEGE PRESIDENTS SPEAK

WHAT YOU HAVE A RIGHT TO EXPECT FROM COLLEGE AND WHY

E VERY COLLEGE PRESIDENT OPERATES IN a unique context. While the institution might belong to a "class" of institutions, such as Land Grant Universities, private colleges, state universities, or community colleges, each college's situation is different in its history, economic context, alumni pressures, and community expectations—to list a few such areas.

This makes it all the more interesting and compelling that, along with specific differences in program development and learning models, the five presidents I spoke with also agreed strongly on core values and priorities for the services and attitudes that would underlie institutional and student success in the future.

The value that tied all the comments together, in my estimation, was "personalization," the concept that policies, procedures, and practices in the adult-friendly college of the future would anticipate the personal needs and aspirations of the learner—meaning there would be academic and nonacademic services that focus on the learner.

One service that bridged all sectors was advising and support. There was broad agreement that academic advising, as well as nonacademic and peer support would be essential ingredients going forward. Unspoken, but understood was the knowledge that *almost two-thirds of the adult learners who are in on-line and blended programs, and who leave college before graduating, do so for non-academic reasons.*

Another area identified by the presidents was the concept of having convenience for the learner. This included scheduling, overall costs, shortened time to earn the degree because of assessment of prior learning, and having an institutional advocate to help with administrative snafus on a daily basis. When it comes to customer service, think Nordstrom or Amazon in higher education.

Finally, there was broad agreement that everything the college or university did would need to be closely referenced to the outside world, especially employment and job readiness. Common themes were working with employers to align learning outcomes and at the same time recognizing people for advanced placement in their in-house training and development programs.

These five presidents put assessment, support, personalization, great content and alignment with the workplace, and reasonable costs at the heart of the adult-friendly college of the future.

▶ *Ed Klonoski,* president of Charter Oak State College

"There are a series of services and a group of attitudes that make a college, in this case Charter Oak (COSC), the kind of place that will attract and hold on to adult learners.

We assess their prior learning by asking questions about knowledge and achievement that they are bringing with them. That would include real estate exams, military learning, transcripted learning from noncollegiate sources, ACE credit—you name it. We are aggressive in accepting non-collegiate formal learning and we also do portfolio evaluations for informal learning. The plain fact is that students who have their prior learning assessed, stay in school, and graduate at higher rates.

Distance learning is essential because adults can be dollar poor but they are even more "time-poor." Distance learning shifts time requirements and adapts to the learner's schedule needs. It is also asynchronous and cohort-based so that the learner has the flexibility time-wise, but also the benefit of being a member of a social community of other learners in the same course. The cohorts are organized around the work requirements of the given week in that course. It is important to remember that, for most adults returning to college, the backbreaker, even more than the money, is the drive time it takes to get to college and back every week.

Two things make learners unhappy—no mentoring from teachers and no mentoring from peer cohorts. They want to be part of a learning community as well as working with a master faculty member.

Finally, we are low-cost and that's important as well. At the end of the day, most of our learners don't have much money. And they are scared to death of debt. They make a decision to attend based on speed to get the degree and on the cost. And, of course, speed to degree is the other side of the cost coin. This means having the assessment of prior learning for advanced placement and distance learning to facilitate atten-dance, and having the learner spending more time learning and less time driving, are important components to that.

Of course, all those things are important. But after admis-sion, if you asked me what the core of the college was, I'd say it's the advising and the advisor. Advising is the heart and soul of the place. Advisors are the intersection between the stu-dents, their academic plan and their career plan. Even the admissions staff advises to assess the fit between learner and COSC. It is critical to have an advising staff that helps you sort out where you want to go and not just get the forms filled out.

In the end, the decision to return and the reasons why people stay and persist is very personal. They are not shopping for eggs. They are consummating a commitment. People come back to college for lots of reasons. For example, we had an NFL player come through to get a degree. He was very wealthy, all set in every regard. When we asked him why he was coming back, he said, 'because I promised my grandmother that I would before she died.' But most need a better job, a new job, so it's personal because its their life.

As we go forward, we must figure out how to provide high quality services for significantly less cost to the learner. For example, places like Charter Oak will become the educational provider for large corporations. We will recognize their internal training for academic credit as well as accepting other credits through PLA. Then between their tuition reimbursement and the credit, we will be able to keep prices close to the corporate reimbursement rate. The value here is that the main outcome that matters is the employment outcome. This direct relationship that responds to the needs of business and employees is the key in the future.

I also think that you will begin to see private investment in public sector institutions. There are more than 31 million unserved learners out there. Whoever can figure out how to reach them and meet their needs is going to be a winner. So we are looking at a new twist—private investment in the public sector as a way to lower costs, sustain and improve quality, and reach more learners. We'll see what happens." (www.charteroak.edu)

▶ *Joyce Judy,* president of The Community College of Vermont

"The underpinning for us, the core value that we keep in front of us all the time, is to meet students where they are at. People differ. And our primary questions are 'What are your needs? Why are you here?'

The fear factor for learners in the beginning is huge. The goal is to make the initial experience for the learner personal and positive. In other words, not overwhelming. Our goal is to help them get through the logistical stuff so that they can ultimately focus on the learning.

There are several key parts to the logistics involved with coming back to school which are critical to address for each learner. Otherwise, the risks of losing the learner before you even get to the learning skyrocket. We know that making all the information available in a way that learners can hear it and act on it can determine success or failure in the on-boarding process.

Here are some of the critical logistics we deal with.

Vermont is rural, very isolated. How do you take education to the population in a rural state? We provide twelve geographic locations within a reasonable distance of 95 percent of all Vermonters, and, as a result, the chances for face-to-face relationships with our professional staff are very good. The centers are a network. There is no 'main' campus, so everyone is in an equal position.

Of course, technology is critical. But the social factor is even more important when we are beginning the relationship with a learner. After they are launched and learning, the IT and online options are great resources. Some people come into the centers and take both on ground and online courses. For us, online education is a format, not a separate track. The degree is from CCV.

Scheduling is critical. You have to accommodate a wide variety of learner work and personal schedules in the course scheduling process. Online class availability can really help here. For example, veterans can move to online if they are deployed. Or someone who works at night may need an afternoon course. The variations are multiple, and we have to meet the needs of the learners. The key thing is to anticipate and adapt to the reality that the learner is living.

Finances are also a big, big deal. Money is really an emotional issue for people. They are hearing that education is deal that costs tens of thousands of dollars—very expensive.

And they are very afraid of getting in over their heads. Whether it is a company or the person and financial aid, you have to really get with people and help them understand the options. We have FA counselors in every center and we believe that this support is critical to success.

Another area where we invest heavily is academic advising. After we have a learner on board, they get an academic advisor. Our advisors' objective is to establish a personal connection and build a relationship with the learner. To be successful, we need to know where the learner is in her life. Like, what significant life events have occurred over the last few years? And what will happen in the next five years? What combination of courses and services will work for you? What is it that works best for you? Our academic advisors are great listeners.

Assessment of Prior Learning (APL) is also another terrific retention device. For people with significant life and work experience, it can save them time and money. And the one thing that virtually every person who comes through the door says is that they don't want to waste their time and money! APL isn't right for everyone. But older students bring a lot of experiential learning with them. For students who go through it, even if they only get twelve credits, there is a tremendous value addition. APL puts their life in order, confirms their journey into one connected flow. And they can see that they had forgotten or devalued their learning below the value that it really has.

This means that in the beginning we hear their story and figure out the best place to start. For some it is remedial education and for others it might be APL. The key is to get them to chart their course and make it their own. In the end they have to own the course they set with us.

Then, we proceed with our support. Our advising is ongoing; the faculty is incredibly supportive, meeting before and after class and giving out contact information for support away from class. Having practitioners teach is a critical part of what we do. The practical application coupled with the down to earth manner and language that practitioners bring adds a whole different dimension of meaning to what is being taught. You move from knowing something to actually applying it, and that's really important. It leads to much deeper learning. Motivated learners and active practitioners working together can make magic. Advisors and faculty make it work for students.

Connections with employers are also critical to give legitimacy by connecting the capacities we are teaching to the requirements of work. Employers are worried about a number of things. For instance, where will the workforce come from in the face of rising rates of retirement and the need to refill positions? At the same time, traditional entry-level low-paying jobs like cashiers are disappearing. Instead, even today, new entry-level jobs require more and higher-level skills and education. How do we prepare for the higher level of sophistication needed in entry-level jobs? Also, how do we grow our own human resources? Employers want to get people who are proven and good employees and who are local and will remain local. How can we upgrade them?

For example, we have a certified production technician program. It's a national credential program. It is incredibly useful and a great way to up-skill workers and get them on a manufacturing track. Now, that can be the end point or they can then go to Vermont Technical College and get a degree. So there is a choice there that didn't exist before. And there are several good responses to that choice. I support the value of short-term training. And learners who need the job and the money can do the program and then go to work.

But learners also deserve further support and information in order to see and understand future opportunities. They deserve a flexible approach which lets them come and go from higher education as their needs and aspirations dictate. The day of the old degree programs, all lined up on Day One and you take it or leave it, are over.

We want learners to keep the connection with us, keep the door open, so learning over the longer term is always possible.

Here's an example. A recent graduate had to start three different times before he was successful. He was a high school dropout and came from a very troubled family with lots of problems including drugs and alcohol. But he then got a GED. His initial two shots at higher education at CCV didn't work. But the third time was the charm. He is working in substance abuse counseling and now has a degree and is enrolled in Castleton State College as a junior in nursing.

Now, is that a success or a failure?

We stayed with him and he stayed with us, and it finally worked. The reality of learners' needs for flexibility and patience is why the way that the federal government collects student participation data and draws conclusions about quality (IPEDS) drives me crazy. IPEDs has nothing to do with reality. When life gets in the way of learning and learners come and go, is that a failure? No, not for them or for us. We have to work with that reality, even if the government calls it something else. Imagine an emergency-room doctor who only counted and treated patients who could walk into the ER. All the others are turned away. Ridiculous? Of course. But that's the way many government policies and programs treat adult learners and the institutions that serve them." (www.ccv.edu)

▶ Javier Miyares, president of University of Maryland University College

"There are two realities that face all of us in higher education: the unsustainable nature of the academic and business models in place at many institutions and the demand to incorporate new services and features that improve educational outcomes while lowering costs to the learner.

On the first point, the primary challenge revolves around providing a quality education at a cost that is still affordable. This is playing out in an environment where the fixed costs of the traditional academic model continue to escalate even as technology is reducing the cost of quality content and delivery. This is where every institution will have to adapt.

At the risk of oversimplifying my view, I would argue that we often complicate things unnecessarily. A close examination of the old model clearly demonstrates the financial burden that comes with a faculty-centric model, one that is extremely difficult to change on an institution-by-institution basis. The costs associated with the rewards system, the governance system, and the control of the curriculum with assessment of learning by departments and individual faculty members, are compounded by the costs inherent in supporting a vertical system of student life from the freshman year forward. In many cases, the institution is in effect supporting a small city with all its attendant services. That approach is bound to become more difficult for many colleges and universities, as well as state legislatures, to support.

A further problem is that some private and most public institutions are more than colleges; they are also employment centers. In many communities, they represent the largest employer offering good benefits and stable jobs. Yet higher education costs are largely driven by payroll, and becoming more efficient means using fewer people to produce more services at lower costs. It will become progressively more difficult to stand up the human resources needed to staff the libraries, the financial aid office, and other services under the old model. But doing things better and cheaper can result in supporting fewer jobs. How can an institution respond responsibly if its plays both the employment role and the educational role?

A second challenge involves the regulatory environment at the state level, as well as the demands of regional accreditation and the US Department of Education. In Maryland, one of the traditional assumptions that underlies the system is the notion that central planning can organize programs in a way that there will be no competition among institutions—the objective being to avoid "costly duplication." That worked reasonably well when books were the medium for learning and campuses were the only places where education could occur. But the advent of the internet challenges that logic by making content available anywhere and anytime by players beyond the reach of state regulatory bodies.

The situation is further complicated by the reality that competition drives innovation. In the central planning model, if there is less competition, there is less incentive for institutions to innovate. The academic enterprise, then, is caught in a new iron triangle populated at each turn by federal and state regulatory bodies and regional accreditors, which together have the effect of stifling innovation both as an aspiration as well as a requirement for survival.

One startling example of this came in the September 2017 report from the US Department of Education's Office of the Inspector General, which recommended that Western Governors University return more than $700 million in federal financial aid—a certain death sentence!—because its teaching model failed to adhere to a traditional definition of faculty. While regional accrediting agencies are changing their standards to allow for innovation, they are ultimately constrained by federal and state regulations.

Finally, there is the challenge of remaining competitive. For UMUC, volume—the number of students we serve—is critical, and scalability is key. It allows us to do things that we otherwise could not. Related to that, how do we take our online tradition and differentiate ourselves from other online institutions? We operate in a competitive marketplace with many other public, for-profit, and private institutions such as Southern New Hampshire University, Western Governors University, Arizona State University and University of Phoenix.

For us, the way to remain competitive is to continually improve the quality of our approaches to teaching and learning, in particular by ensuring that our graduates' skills align with workplace needs. With a laser-like focus on student learning and success, we believe technology is the answer. There is no way to increase quality and volume while remaining affordable without major and continuing investments in technology across the learner experience and all institutional functions.

On the academic side, the question is this: If we can break free from yesterday's practices, what should we be doing differently to serve new types of learners with higher quality and lower costs? To make a long story short—and perhaps concern some traditionalists at the same time—the answer goes beyond pursuing academic excellence. The very definition of excellence needs to be recast in student-centric ways. In our new and emerging world, the overall user experience for higher education in the online and digital universe must be *superb*.

Adult learners have a right to expect great student services that are tailored to their needs, available when they need them, and delivered in a mode that is friendly to their circumstances. This includes personal and academic advising, career information and placement, Amazon-style accessibility, and overall quality of service in troubleshooting daily institutional issues. Higher education tends to approach retention as a student problem, rather than looking at itself and analyzing which aspects of the way it does business get in the way of student success. For example, a student who cannot get timely answers to basic questions about academic programs and services (such as financial aid) is much more likely to fail—no matter how well academically prepared she or he may be. I recall observing a student focus group and hearing one participant say, "I have a lot of problems in my life. When I come to school, I don't need you to give me more. I don't need to be given the runaround when I ask basic questions about my program, financial aid, or other university requirements."

When it comes to academic programs, we need to provide a straight academic path that can be compressed when the student brings validated prior learning to the program. Importantly, the cost to the learner is more than simply establishing lower costs and price points. Time is money, and if a learner can complete a program in less time and still achieve the desired learning outcomes, so much the better.

Most adult learners are very practical. They want a promotion, a new career, or a better job. And they need to be able see and understand college's payoff in these terms—and see it clearly—in order to make practical decisions about its value. Lower costs and less time to degree combine to make the journey more attractive, work more acceptable, and completion more valuable to the learner.

If we pay attention, our business processes can also have a positive effect on student success. For example, allowing students to enroll late may sound good. There is just one problem. In most cases, late enrollments don't work. Data clearly shows that having time to plan for your academic life, fitting it into an already busy personal and work life, and getting good academic advice—in fact, just having a chance to reflect on what you are about to do—is tremendously important. Offering students opportunities to test out a learning environment before plunging in is another way to help them adapt to their new reality.

We can also help incoming students by developing program plans that are more focused, with *fewer* course choices and more emphasis on what they need to be successful after they graduate. Choice can be a killer, and it is far better to be practical with adult learners. This means fewer electives and a more structured curriculum in which the courses offered are driven by student needs, not faculty interest in specific topics, and there is greater investment in those services that support early success.

Some might argue that these things have little if anything to do with the classroom—but they are nonetheless critical to success. Classroom and curricular design, teaching and assessment, asynchronous environments and data analytics— *all* are critical. But even if they are done very well and are vital to survival, they are still not enough to guarantee success in this new and highly competitive marketplace. The human touch is still important, and what humans do helps students learn how to think, though it has evolved from simply serving as a purveyor of content. As in journalism, academic content is becoming free (witness the increasing support for open educational resources, or OERs). The role of the faculty is changing, too, from that of a content expert to more of a mentor and guide who fosters critical thinking and helps students learn *how* to learn.

The past twenty years have shown that changes in adult higher education find their way into institutions that serve traditional students. For example, the use of technology, particularly online education, is no longer the province of adult-serving institutions. Similarly, the use of OERs; the emphasis on increasing student preparation for the workforce; the use of analytics to track learner progress and to manage for increased efficiency; the shift to straighter degree paths with fewer electives; the development of more powerful articulations between two- and four-year colleges; the practice of granting college credit for non-classroom learning; and the evolving role of the faculty—all were first embraced by colleges and universities serving adult students and can now be expected to "bleed" into other institutions. Strong evidence suggests that competition leads to innovation across segments. As increasing numbers of first-generation students from increasingly diverse backgrounds enroll, the lessons

learned in the adult education market will become ever more relevant to traditional institutions across our nation and around the world."
(www.umuc.edu)

▶ *Chris Bustamante,* president of Rio Salado College

"The key to serving adults successfully is to be a place that is focused on the learners' needs, not the institution's needs. You need to be a team and an institution where the learners know that you care.

That means having programs and resources that adapt to learners and their needs. These include assessment of prior learning, proper placement, and a lot more handholding in the beginning. Also, we have 48 start dates a year, and that flexibility is a big draw for learners. And we focus on affordability as well at only $86 per credit hour.

Sometimes you only have one shot. Having finally gotten their nerve up to come to the college, we better have people ready to serve the learner and attempt to meet their needs.

The question is: Are you building a culture that is instinctively responsive to learners' needs and realities. We have veterans' services, language services, and advising to help students explore learning and career pathways. We have to show them we care and can help them get where they want to go.

In the workforce area, we are preparing people for jobs they don't have. Or maybe they need a promotion within their current environment, so we are up-skilling. About 80 percent of our work is credential work—last year we had 750 degrees and over 4000 credentials of all kinds that included licensure and teacher certs and then linking them to employers.

In the coming world, the link to employment is going to be way deeper than a career fair. There are direct content linkages that can be integrated into certificate programs and then linked to industry exams. This way employment and qualifications are integrated with the program, not something that happens afterwards. Apprentice programs are coming back as well. But the underlying value to all approaches is that the outcomes are predetermined and agreed-upon, so there is less doubt and chance to miss the alignment with the job that exists.

For example, Kroger wanted an option to meet the needs of their shift workers in retail management. They are willing to cover the costs, assist with the curriculum development, and promote participation to their employees. This program is designed to be all for credit and crafted to the needs of the company or industry. Then, with proper preparation and some analytics, you can transfer the competencies into other programs. This means there can be an internal or external career path. You are not trapped in one path necessarily because of the college credit you have already earned because it can be transferred to other career paths and opportunities.

Looking forward, companies will continue to have technologies that will be way ahead of us and more sophisticated than anything we can afford. Why not work with some of those companies, using their technologies, to get educational opportunities in front of people? Like a Netflix Channel and app for Rio Salado? You could do it on an open basis where people study and then find a home institution. Or, you could do individual institutional applications. So instead of just having *Game of Thrones* available in your living room, you could also have a bevy of college services to choose from.

We are going to have to reach beyond our online framework and LMSs to harnessing the power of the private sector, use the home screen, choose courses, chat. Now, that would truly be a free-range learning network.

Also, using data analytics, you will see the wholesale mobility and transfer of competencies from work to learning to work. It's all the same information, and we can apply it in multiple settings and situations to serve the learner and the employer better. That will also allow us to convert to credit other learning options that are available from non-campus sources. In a world of low cost or free content, we will be upselling assessment as a bridge to certificates and degrees.

Finally, I think you will see some colleges, like Rio Salado, act as the trusted online service provider, behind the scenes, for other colleges that don't have the money or the expertise to stand the program up for themselves."
(www.riosalado.edu)

▶ *Paul LeBlanc*, president, Southern New Hampshire University

"In my view, a 'Learning Friendly College' is organized to help 'unstick' learners and propel them towards their goals. Think about the underlying obstacles to success.

- Cost. Cost is always a consideration. Learners often have limited resources and need A) to know they can afford the education and B) that their investment is worth it, that it will pay off.
- Convenience. Adult learners are busy people with busy lives. They are working and trying to fit in education along with jobs and family. Online learning is convenient compared to synchronous, hybrid and campus modes.
- Completion time. Time is the 'other' expense. Learners increasingly want to know how long it will take to get to the finish line. They are often stuck and feel some sense of urgency—that's why

they are finally willing to go back to school. This encourages practices such as the nine-week term, assessment of prior learning, and transfer credit-friendliness

- The Credential. Learners want to know its value in the workplace. Will it change the trajectory of my life?

The interplay between these qualities, taken together, lead to the broad structural shape of the program. And 'learner-friendly' addresses the situations and issues that the adult learner faces.

ON LEARNER SUCCESS

Learner success, however, although connected to friendliness, is driven by other things. I believe that the critical factor in increasing student success is advising. This includes a good CRM (Customer Relationship Management System), a proactive advising model, and good advisor/learner ratios. But advising also must address nonacademic factors, such as 'how can I fit studying in?' and the emotional and psychological baggage (confidence is a big one) that adult learners often bring with them. 'How do I handle the conflicting demands of family, learning, and work logistics and time?' We need to remember that two thirds of our dropouts do so for nonacademic reasons. Online learning can be isolating. We have to continually reinforce community and personal support.

BRINGING THE TWO TOGETHER

Everything I think about and, ultimately, do is based on the following premise. The impact of technology is already asserting itself in profound ways. People in traditional higher education who think they can duck its implications are making a huge mistake.

- There will be more intelligence in systems. And, to simplify the matter, we will be moving from dumb systems and smart people to smart people and smarter systems.

- Personalized learning pathways will become a core operating reality. And the university will evolve from being the conductor (rigid and on track) to the curator of individualized education plans (IEPs) that are flexible and adaptable and personalized).

- The experience of learning itself will be profoundly changed by virtual reality, artificial intelligence, and immersive technology.

- We will experience a remapping of cognitive skills, like what happened after writing was invented. In that long-term evolution, we went from relying completely on our memory (what we knew literally equaled what we could remember) to now knowing where to look for information, because for the first time it was written down and stored somewhere. Now, going forward, machine-assisted exploration will give us new cognitive tools. Think about an "Alexa" for learning support. This is an interesting question to consider for knowledge creation and transfer.

- The GPS for learning and work is coming, and higher education must either adapt or become marginalized. Why would we continue to think that a model based on committing 4-6 percent of your life span (as those approach one hundred years) in one chunk to further your education will work in the future? Look at UDEMY (www.udemy.com) and its 10M users. There you see people teaching people in the early stages of a future-oriented model. The EQUIP program, which I helped design, is a good example of this. It is a signal from the future.

- Watch 'digital natives,' the people under twenty who are growing up today. They turn to YouTube for everything. They are visual, and they are immersive.

The point here is not that the model of the future is known and predictable. It is exactly the opposite. The models will be multiple and variable. And the drivers of those models, the characteristics of their practices and procedures, and the resources available in the broad society to support them will define and determine learner friendliness and success." (www.snhu.edu)

Taken collectively, these comments give you a shopping list for the services, terms, and conditions you should expect from the "adult-friendly college" of the future. And an informed consumer is a more powerful consumer.

THE EMERGING GPS FOR LEARNING AND WORK

INTRODUCTION

EVERY NEW CAR AND MOBILE phone has a GPS travel application that tells you how to get from where you are to your destination in the most efficient and direct way. Of course if you decide to take a more scenic route, there are always the second and third options offered. Whichever route you choose, however, you are secure in knowing that the information, the directions, and the time involved is essentially accurate and dependable.

The same kind of flexibility and focus is coming to educational planning and career preparation. Whether you are an independent learner, an adult looking for the right college, a first-time job seeker, someone unemployed and trying get back to work, or a career-switcher, these new services will support your quest. Elements of a GPS for learning and work have been evolving online over the last few years, enriching the space previously occupied primarily by adult-friendly colleges and their services.

New services include thousands of free courses offered online from several university consortia. They also include formal education and training programs that operate outside of college sponsorship and services that help you research career alternatives and then find educational programs that meet their requirements

When you are finished with section three, you will have a clear understanding of the types of resources that are available to you as an adult learner. You will have looked at and hopefully sampled the different tools and services that are right for you at this point in your life. And, if you choose to, you can begin to learn actively either independently or with a learning partner.

6

CRACKING THE CODE
GETTING TO THE RIGHT COLLEGE OR CREDENTIALS

THINK BACK TO "THE SCARECROW'S DILEMMA" which we discussed in chapter 3. As should be obvious by now, millions of people share the Scarecrow's predicament when it comes to colleges and employers. And you don't need a brain. You already have one of those! What you do need is the recognition of your hidden credentials and, as the presidents underscored earlier, support services which are sympathetic and responsive to your needs as an adult learner.

When colleges and employers don't recognize them, they are denying you the benefits and the power that would naturally flow from your hidden credentials. Beyond being gross knowledge discrimination, this is a wasteful and destructive practice in several respects for the following reasons:

- It buries the value of your learning and hides that learning from all who would benefit.
- It demeans adults who have significant personal learning and who want to benefit from its worth.

- It perpetuates the connections between self-esteem and confidence on the one hand and formal educational attainment on the other.
- It transforms college from a learning experience into a hunt for the credential, "that piece of paper."

Assessing your experiential learning sounds complicated. And although doing so in a collegiate setting for academic credit is a demanding process, there is really no reason why you can't begin the process informally, personally identifying your personal learning and hidden credentials. In fact, it can be quite simple and fun. If you want to practice a little before starting, try keeping a diary for two or three weeks. Write a page a day on what you did during the last 24 hours and how you feel about it. Then read it all back to see the richness in action, situations, and feelings that those weeks contained.

There are additional informal ways that you can begin learning to do the same thing. They are not, however, something that you should rush through. To get true value, each exercise should take several hours and each should also inform the others. Why? Because learning how to remember what you did and reflect on what it meant to you, what you learned and how you changed as a result, is not a quick walk to the corner store. It lies at the core of your cracking the code and identifying your hidden credentials, all the learning that you have done. So plan on a slower, more deliberate hike.

The exercises include:

- Taking ten coins out of your pocket and lining them up sequentially by date of issue. Then, recall and write down major events that occurred in each year represented by those dates. This is a good way to crack the wall that keeps you from remembering your personal learning as Allen Tough described. This slightly random exercise will not only help you begin to remember events, but also to see the reality of "forgetting" your personal learning.

- Developing a timeline of important events and significant experiences in your life beginning with graduation from high school. The timeline will help you remember what you were doing year by year and that, in turn, will help you remember still more detail.
- Thinking and writing about what these significant experiences meant to you, how they affected you, how you reacted to them— both positively and negatively.
- Thinking and listing the learning resources you used in specific instances—books, MOOCs, podcasts, Facebook videos, articles, DVDs, and others. Did you learn alone, or with others? Did you learn at work informally or in a professional development exercise? Did you have a coach or a tutor?
- Thinking about the events and instances that you have accumulated on your timeline from the perspective of roles and responsibilities that you held, and analyzing them for increasing complexity and how doing them changed you as a person.
- Writing an autobiographical, "What's It All About, Alfie?" essay on your life to date. This is the way that you can begin to reconstruct your personal learning journey, the path that has led to your current circumstances and created your hidden credentials.[13]

Then, if you decide that you want to go further, check out the two URLs listed below. They are two examples of resources that will give you a quick answer to whether you can benefit from assessing your experiential learning.

- The Kaplan Calculator is very simple and quick. It is aimed at simply giving you an indication of whether assessing your prior learning is a something you should look into. (www.portfolio.kaplan.edu/calculator)
- The CAEL PLA Accelerator is more thorough and aimed at giving you a more comprehensive understanding of your

prior learning and prior learning assessment. (www.cael.
org/higher-education/pla-accelerator)

Taken together, they will whet your appetite for a journey of
reflection and discovery.

As one powerful example of the value of this journey, listen to
Phil Barrett recount how he developed a portfolio of his prior
learning, got academic recognition for it, and the deep learning
and satisfaction that he received as a result. Phil was able to remember what he did, what it meant to him, and how he changed
over his adult lifetime. He got these understandings and perceptions because he went through a formal process at a local college
in which he collected, analyzed and self-assessed his personal
learning with a trained faculty member.

And, as you read Phil's story, remember Allen Tough's research
that identified adult learning projects and the fact that most people forget about their personal learning and it sits there "hiding
on plain sight."

▶ *Phil Barrett*

Phil knew that if he was going to be promoted to his boss's job when
the time came, a bachelor's degree would be a distinct advantage
even though he had years of experience and thousands of hours
invested in management training. Phil needed to find a college that
would enable him to learn during the evening and on weekends and
give him credit for the learning he had done on the job over the
years, to recognize his hidden credentials. But he didn't realize how
great the satisfaction or deep the learning would be.

"My boss was talking about retiring in a few years, and I
wanted to sit in his chair. His job description required a bachelor's degree. Since I got my associate degree, I had spent my
time taking classes that were convenient: one-week seminars

and one-day workshops. I had accumulated all this time and experience and never got any credit for it.

I discovered that there was a college near-by that would consider giving you credit for learning you had done outside of school, so I looked into it and saw what was available. The program made a big difference for me because of the credit that I received. But, beyond getting the credit, it changed the way I thought about things.

As I got more into the program, I found out that I knew more than I thought I did. I started listing all the things I had done in my life, and I suddenly realized that I had done more than I thought I had. The writing helped me remember, and it brought all my learning back up to the surface. I think we lose knowledge because we aren't challenged to use it. Much of what I know is in the back of my mind. It just needed to surface.

I'm not the type of person who believes that anybody owes me anything. If I get something, I want to feel as if I've earned it. The assessment program is all about what you learned away from school. It's not just what you have done or experienced, but what you learned as a result. That's the important part. They didn't give me credit for just being there. I had to be able to prove that I learned it.

The learning assessment program also taught me how to see the difference between something I did and how I changed as a result. For instance, I thought about how I used to react to a certain type of supervision from my boss when I started work. Then, when I got up to be a supervisor, I observed others' management styles and how I reacted to the task. I was able to see a change in myself. I could say, 'Hey, I can see where I went from being this type of person to that type.' Or, I could see when I started thinking about my responsibilities as a manager rather than just being a manager. I realized what it really meant and what I had to do."

Phil discovered a great store of personal learning that he had forgotten about until he began to formally explore his own bodies of knowledge in the portfolio course. Then as he recalled and valued the learning he had done, he got more than academic recognition for their experience factor. He gained insight and sophistication because he learned how to reflect on his experience. When you know how to actively reflect, you can separate what you have done, your experience, from what you have learned and how you have changed as a result, your personal learning. And your steadily accumulating personal learning adds up to your hidden credentials, your key to more successful living.

Phil found the experience to be far deeper and more profound as a personal learning experience than he had ever anticipated. When you add those values to saving time and money on the way to getting your degree, that is a great deal!

OTHER RESOURCES THAT WILL HELP YOU "CRACK THE CODE"

The Council for the Assessment of Experiential Learning (CAEL) is the national leader in several areas including assessment of your prior learning and identifying colleges that offer other "adult-friendly" services to smooth your path to and through college.

CAEL's LearningCounts program helps to assess prior learning and to find a college that will accept it. (www.learningcounts.org) LearningCounts serves institutions which have agreed to accept prior learning that has been assessed by CAEL.

Finding colleges that are organized with your needs in mind is important. And, as you learned from the college presidents' interviews in the last chapter, there are colleges which have been designed with your needs specifically in mind. In addition to the colleges featured in chapter 5, and although it is not a comprehensive list, institutions that are CAEL members and participants in LearningCounts (www.learningcounts.com/portfolio-assessment/

fn/) are good places to start the search. (www.cael.org/about-us/ membership/cael-members)

Other services that can help you get value for your learning outside of college and find the college that is right for you include:

- The College Navigator (www.nces.ed.gov/collegenaviga- tor/). This is a simple search engine that allows you to en- ter all your personal preferences re college and then find colleges that match up with your expressed needs and preferences. If you find a college from this list that is also a CAEL or Learning Counts member, that is a good pre- liminary indicator that it is an "adult-friendly" institution.
- The American Council on Education's assessment of mili- tary and corporate training courses for academic credit (www2.acenet.edu/credit/?) and the National College Credit Recommendation Service at the University of the State of New York. (www.nationalccrs.org/) These organi- zations evaluate courses that are offered in non-collegiate settings for academic equivalency and credit. They are ex- cellent sources for verifying whether courses you have taken during your military service or at work have aca- demic value if and when you seek further education.

THE EDPUNKS' GUIDE

One other excellent resource describing learning services is *The Edupunks' Guide to a DIY Credential*.[14] (www.diyubook.com) This is a different, but highly reputable source of programs, exercises, and institutions that will help you gain clear focus on the options available and the best path forward for you.

As Anna Kamenetz has indicated in *The Edupunks' Guide*, there are a whole slew of new programs and services which put you in touch with courses and alternative pathways to a credential that may meet your needs with or without a college program.

Next, we will describe examples of two types of programs that offer you courses, free or low cost and on demand, as well as access to micro-credentials and degrees and services that offer new pathways to work which may or may not involve college.

As you read, you will notice similarities among these programs. You will also notice distinct differences. Think of your exploration as being like you were shopping for a new pair of shoes. Given what you are looking for, the fit has to be right. What these new resources, as well as the services and pathways described in the last two chapters, give you is the chance for a far better fit with your needs and aspirations. No more "one size fits all."

These are not the only programs and services that exist in this space, not by a long shot. They are, however, programs that I have come to admire as representative of the coming GPS for learning and work.

COURSES, CREDENTIALS, AND MICRO-CREDENTIALS

Straighterline

Listen to Burck Smith, StraighterLine's founder, describe his original thinking and the current state of the business. (www.straighterline.com)

> "I began planning for StraighterLine in 2006 and launched it in 2008. StraighterLine represented an extension of the thinking I had been doing since my graduate work in the mid-90s. The notion was to offer fifty to sixty of the most common and popular general education courses online and at a price much closer to their true cost of delivery. General education courses represent about 1/3 of all course enrollments and are largely the same across most colleges. Further, these courses are already heavily transferred between high schools and colleges and among colleges.

From the very beginning we did *not* want to be accredited. For colleges, accreditation provides their students access to free and cheap money with which to pay tuition, some level of credit transferability and an imprimatur of quality in a crowded market place. However, accreditation also requires the delivery of an entire degree program rather than pieces, an administrative and faculty oversight structure that may not be useful, required layers of student service that may be unnecessary for individual students and the whole vertical stack of functions that comprise the traditional college structure. All of this keeps costs and prices high and makes it difficult to "unbundle" the college structure. That's what we wanted to do.

In order for us to succeed, we needed to replicate the functions of accreditation without being accredited. First, we kept prices really low so that financial aid was less of an issue. Second, we created guaranteed credit transfer agreements with willing colleges to ensure interoperability. Lastly, we had our courses reviewed and recommended by the American Council on Education's Credit Recommendation Service to provide the "Good Housekeeping Seal of Approval" for market validation.

Our initial value proposition to colleges was that we could be a free source of new enrollments that are very likely to persist to a degree. That has worked. In addition, we've found that some colleges are referring students needing prerequisites or at-risk students to us to take a handful of courses. We work with the referring college to return those referred students. This means that for colleges we help them grow enrollment, conversion and retention. For students, we lower their cost and risk of completing their degree."

Here's what some of the StraighterLine "alumni" have to say.

▶ *Jason Ransom*

"I did not come from a traditional school experience. I dropped out of HS in my sophomore year and ended up working full time. Perhaps it was a lack of discipline or my parent's tumultuous relationship. Either way, it was a survival mode for me from early on.

In the first phase of my career, I was fortunate to secure a job in a medical hospital. I was a nurse's aide. This was a glamorous title with activities centered around cleaning operating rooms, stocking cabinets, and running for blood. Fortunately, the environment, in addition to the surgeons and nurses, consisted of medical sales reps that over time took me under their wing.

Eventually, one of them recommended me for an entry position as a support rep for a major medical device company. Due to my relationship and being recommended, no one asked about my education.

Understanding the blessing of this moment in my career, I attacked this opportunity with a laser focus to outwork everyone. The return on this effort came with a series of promotions over the next fifteen years as I progressed through the corporate ladder with key leadership positions in management.

The turning point for me didn't come at work. It came at home. I have four kids and they began to ask about college in an effort to start on a plan for their future. But I couldn't help them in an authentic way because it was not a journey I had experienced. It really weighed heavily on me that I would not be able to be a role model for them when it came to earning a degree. It was a journey that I had not taken. I wanted to not just give them good advice but also be a key example for them.

So I began looking at options. Going to a campus was out of the question, so online was the best for me. After doing research on available options, I learned about StraighterLine and registered. My first course for credit was medical terminology, and I passed it. Then I began to lay out a roadmap on this important project. I quickly fell in love with the structure and it really suited me personally.

Thomas Edison State University is a StraighterLine partner. This means StraighterLine courses have been approved by the American Council of Education, and Thomas Edison honored that approval. Fortunately everything I did at StraighterLine was good at Edison. I checked on the best partner for me in terms of advanced placement, and it was them because I could basically challenge for the degree if I had the knowledge. I took a lot of courses with Straighter-Line, with a few additional resources from CLEP (www.clep.collegeboard.org) and ALEKS (www.ALEKS.com) utilizing their credit transfer through ACE (American Council of Education) and then challenged for the degree at Edison.

At this point in my career, I own an international biotech business focused on neuronal repair and protection. This has allowed me the ability to work from home. Through this work structure, I was able to maximize key available time toward chipping away at completing my degree

The whole process took a year and consisted of extreme self-discipline, many late nights in the books and a requirement to truly know the material by successfully passing countless proctored exams. The experience was very exhilarating and incredibly rewarding once completed.

One of the many things that I love about StraighterLine is that it allows you to be bold in your aspirations and save time and money. The financial saving is a significant part, very doable, and the ability to compress time is spectacular. Even if you have the will, a traditional college won't allow you to do either of those things.

The StraighterLine/Edison partnership is great for someone who has some additional 'tribal' knowledge. There is great power in being able to combine strong life experience, activity-based experience, and knowledge.

After I finished, I started entertaining the idea of going further, like getting a master's or an MBA. So after extensive research, I called Western Governors University and enrolled. I was so well equipped because of the experience I gained at StraighterLine that I soared at Western Governors. I am just finishing a Masters in Science in Management and Leadership and an MBA. Because several of the courses will count towards both degrees, I'll have both completed within a year.

Now other passions that I had previously shelved are beginning to creep from the back of my mind. As with my core focus to assist my kids in their development into becoming young leaders, I have always carried a burning desire to circle back and help kids coming from similar environments—through mentorship, personal development, and structured guidance. The balance I gained between overcoming the obstacles in my childhood and my 21st-century education drives me to spark those young brains that will bring special value to the world through their gifts to shape the future."

▶ Sheila Ann Jordan

Sheila is a feisty, straightforward woman who has known that she wanted not only a BS, but also an MBA, from an early age. As so often happens, however, she got thrown offtrack by several factors that can disrupt the learning path—a poor fit with her first college, high costs at her second college, and then the complications of life, marriage, motherhood, and work. But she never gave up.

"I am forty-eight years old. As a little kid I dreamed of going to college. The only person in my family who had graduated college was my aunt Sarah. I went on campus with her when I was very young and had that dream from then on!

In 1987, I graduated from high school and went directly to college. I did well, but I transferred after a year because I didn't like the school. So I went to another college and really liked it. After I made it through a year successfully, I had to leave. It was too expensive.

Then life intervened. Marriage, work, kids, and twenty-five years flew by. I took a course here or there and kept looking for a college that would fit me and my needs. It wasn't working out, but I never lost that yearning for an MBA.

Then along came high quality, online, and free courses, the MOOCs, and I began to interact with that world. As I did that, I eventually learned about StraighterLine. I checked it out, and it looked really good for me. You paid a low monthly subscription fee and you could take as many courses as you wanted. The courses were approved by the ACE and were accepted by partner colleges. So I went to my last college, but they said "no" because they weren't a partner. But a year later, they became a partner! I went back to my academic advisor and made an academic plan that would be accepted by my university, Franklin University.

Now, you've got to remember that I had a full-time job, was a mother of two, and ran a nonprofit and a coaching business on the side. I was busy (!) *and* didn't have a lot of money. StraighterLine was perfect for me because of the subscription policy and the flex time. I could go as fast or as slow as I wanted, and I could do the work whenever my schedule allowed it.

When we got it all organized, my plan included one CLEP test, eleven courses from StraighterLine, and two required courses at Franklin. Having waited twenty-nine years, I was anxious to start and finish! I started by taking and passing the CLEP in April 2016, then immediately started the Straighter-Line classes. In September 2016, I transferred my Straighter-Line credits, and enrolled at Franklin University in Columbus, Ohio, for my last semester. I graduated in December 2016.

The trick was to find the right bridging mechanism to get from where I was to where I wanted to be, Franklin University. And that was StraighterLine. The courses were on a par with others I had taken and the flexibility was awesome.

The whole thing is sort of like an education hack—I was able to save the money to pay for the more expensive courses at Franklin University because I was saving so much and moving so fast with StraighterLine.

If I hadn't found StraighterLine, none of this would have happened. Now I think of myself as a success story that was waiting to happen. But it couldn't happen until Straighter-Line changed the rules. I was determined and resilient, always thinking and looking until I found the right handle.

Now, I am fulfilling a lifelong intention to get an MBA. Franklin University has online programs for both the MBA and at the doctoral level. I've enrolled, and have two semesters of the MBA program to go. When I finish my master's degree in May, I intend to enroll in the Doctoral Program. There's no stopping me! In five years, I plan to have my doctorate, and leave my full-time job, and run my businesses full-time. Then I plan to teach adult learners.

My oldest daughter graduated from Duke in May 2015. I wanted to beat her to a degree, but that didn't happen. Now she's about to get a second degree, a BSN. My younger daughter is graduating from high school in 2018. We'll graduate together. (She smiles.) Then, she is off to college!

I love the notion of hidden credentials. I had an amazing career in the nonprofit and for-profit world and was able to do some things usually only available to people with a degree. I've learned a lot. The things that I learned while working and parenting helped enormously when I returned to school. They made me a better student—committed and intentional, with a laser-beam focus on the goal!"

edX

The organization edX is a consortium of institutions including MIT, Harvard, Berkeley, and the University System of Maryland as well as many international institutions. (www.edx.org)

It started as a provider of free courses from its member institutions, and edX has evolved into an independent learner's paradise with course sequences focused on continuous lifelong learning as well as career-relevant content. So you can take courses and programs for personal gain and enrichment. Or you can also take courses and earn certificates to demonstrate knowledge and determination, either for academic and professional success or recognition. edX portends "free-range learning" in a learner-centered world. And if this approach suits you, you can be the driver of your own learning.

As CEO Anant Agarwal said in an interview, "Learners are moving away from the "top down" approach, represented by parents, colleges, and employers dictating what they do. And they are moving towards a more "horizontal" approach in which they work independently, directing and curating their own learning. And edX is moving with them."

▶ Danaka Porter

Danaka had a very different journey than many of the people you have met on these pages. A college graduate with a great job, from the outside her career looked as if it were off to a great start. But then reality intruded.

> "After I graduated from university in 2010, I got some awesome work experience and moved up to a VP position at a business in Calgary. I always wanted to get my master's degree. I was thinking that it would be very cool to bring "outside "business experience—I'm into supply chain management—into the classroom as a part-time faculty member sometime in my fu-

ture. And I wanted to be able to move up at work. So to do all that, I needed at least a master's degree. But the school commitment, in terms of time and money, was impossible to negotiate. I needed to work and I couldn't do both. So I had a great job, but I was stuck.

Then, after about five years of working, I lost my job—got laid off just like that, bang! That was the kick in the pants that I needed to bring school into my working life one way or the other. So, out of necessity, I became a self-employed consultant, got a few contracts, and began to network looking for college opportunities.

I knew a guy from MIT, and I was networking with him and others, looking for learning options that would fit my life and my wallet. He turned me on to a supply chain management series of courses through edX that led to a MicroMasters certificate. The MicroMasters® is a program where you earn a certificate MIT gives after you pass five courses and a two-part, six-hour exam that validates your learning up to that point. The deal was that if you completed these, then you could apply to MIT using the grades from the five courses and exam. And, if you got accepted, you go to campus in Boston for five to six months and finish the master's degree and your dissertation.

So, I signed up for courses taught by MIT faculty at edX (www.edx.org) in the supply chain management curriculum of the MicroMasters program, a cool new "bite-by-bite" approach to the masters where you don't try to do the whole thing at once. The technology was incredible, smooth as butter, like going to college with an Amazon user experience. The whole program was on one platform—very fluid and really amazing. You were with learners from all over the world—talking, collaborating, sharing experiences, discussing real-world experiences and problems we were all having at work. So its value was way more than the course itself; it created a community. Very cool. We still have a discussion forum on Facebook and continue to share constantly. We are connected.

All this cost $150 per course. And it was MIT!! Very self-directed. The lectures were released every week, so there was a sequence and a structure to the assignments. If you needed help, there were peers, TAs, and, as a last resort, the professor. It was all very well-balanced and easy to schedule.

You come to a crossroads in your life. In my case it was losing my job. And you want to go in a new direction, but you're trapped. Then I found this answer and I am in the middle of a work and learning journey as we speak.

So you get the MicroMasters certificate if you pass the courses online and then pass a really nasty, six-hour exam. Even if I don't proceed to the on-campus master's program, two things are clear.

First, having the MicroMasters is a big deal. Already I am subcontracted out to the Canadian Navy and Coast Guard to help them with shipbuilding. It has bumped me up to a whole new level with work. And, the job offers I am getting are incredible. I have far more confidence in my own ability and capacity. I am trusted much more highly and my professional instincts are way, way better.

Second, if I still want a masters at some point, there are a ton of other options down the road with online and blended programs. So either way, I am in the driver's seat.

The way that MIT is doing this changes the way adults can think about higher education. They bring education into your life without asking you to slam on the brakes, sit at a desk, stop working, and listen to someone talk at you. That's nuts. They bridged the gap and allowed me to go straight ahead and get what I need. I could literally learn something in the morning and use it in the afternoon at work.

As for the time involved if I went to MIT, I would be gone for only five to six months, not two years. That works. Take a leave of absence, go do it, and come back. Not only is it way cheaper than a two-year program. You can see the end and the payoff before you begin. You have a much higher degree of control. It is a very concrete feeling. I have known from last March exactly what I needed to do to qualify. And if I qualify I will know exactly what I can expect when I get there.

This pathway, even if getting laid off forced me onto it, has given me much more control over my time, my life, my career, and my career trajectory. I make more money and have more freedom than before. It gave me power and an attitude towards life and work that I didn't have before."

▶ Marisol Moran

Marisol Moran is a classic free-range learner. Not because she is like all the others, but because she uses edX to learn what she wants when she wants to learn it. In her case, the courses she took influenced her direction and decision-making in a more traditional college setting.

"I always enjoyed the traditional model of education, liked the interaction in class and all that. But one summer after I had graduated from college, I took a philosophy course on edX just for fun, to see what it was like. And I liked it a lot. But I didn't do anything with it.

Then, when I was in graduate school at the Middlebury Institute of International Studies (MIIS) in Monterey, California, I was studying to get a master's degree in public administration (MPA) with an emphasis in program evaluation and impact. But when I took another edX course in that area to supplement what I was getting at MIIS, I realized that I wasn't as excited about that angle as I was about another option in the program: organizational development, marketing, and branding. At least that's what I sensed.

So I took two more courses with edX that supplemented that option and found that it really was where I wanted to spend my time and put my energy. And I went whole hog in that direction, finishing with my CapStone project which focused completely on branding.

Now, after graduation, I am focusing on social media marketing as well. When I get enough money together, I'll probably go back and take some courses in that area as well and get a certificate. But, to date, edX has been instrumental in helping me think and work my way through the series of decisions that led me to the place, professionally, where I am now.

The dimensions that the courses opened and the value they added were immeasurable. I'm a little nervous to go on the platform because I always see something that I want to pursue, but I have to be careful with my time."

Marisol used edX to try things out, to supplement her traditional studies and help her set and solidify a new direction in her professional journey. And she will, in true free-range learner fashion, go back when she wants to, needs to, and has the resources to do so.

THE OPEN EDUCATION CONSORTIUM AND SAYLOR ACADEMY

Two other sources for a wide variety of high-quality course content are the Open Education Consortium (OEC) (www.oeconsortium.org) and Saylor Academy (www.sayloracademy.org).

▶ Mary Lou Forward, OEC

"When I came to OEC, I was coming from being the Dean of African Studies at the School for International Training in Brattleboro, Vermont. I had seen firsthand the disparities in available resources and access to education and programs in

Africa. And it was apparent to me right off the bat that Open Educational Resources (OERs) would be a great source of opportunity for bright people everywhere, but especially in less developed countries, who cannot otherwise get access to resources and education to solve problems.

The big question was access for poor and rural people. So the first job was convincing people to create content, open it, provide it and make it accessible. We went from having 8,000 course resources to over 30,000 very quickly.

So then we shifted from focusing on the scaffolding, the content, to building the house. What will we actually do for people and how do we want the materials to be used? We pivoted pretty quickly from a focus on access to a focus on collaboration. We wanted to create the potential in which our resources could be woven together to serve the particular needs of the learner. We wanted to help people identify and reach their personal goals. We wanted to inspire active learning on the part of the learners.

How are OEC resources used predominantly? There are three pre-dominant ways.

- Faculty and students use OERs in the classroom both to supplement traditional references and also as a primary resource. They are curated materials and as they become integrated with the overall teaching-learning process, they become even more valuable.
- People are also used to turning to the internet to get answers to questions. And higher education still has their confidence as a source of information. So they trust and use information from OEC institutions to learn the things they want to know, to answer their questions.
- And, finally, there is also a broader lifelong learning usage. For example, if a museum is hosting an

exhibit, a diorama on water management, we can add referenced resource material on related water management issues. The message is "Come to us and deepen your learning."

Looking ahead, I believe that the incorporation of digital resources will become mainstream in education as well as other areas. As usage increases, OER usage increases. Then classroom use will increase.

I also anticipate that there will be an increase in the active learning I was discussing earlier. Bringing in diversity of perspective and thought, reviewed through OERs will reach more students, and they will begin to understand that there is a commonality across borders, of problems and areas of study. That opens the door to more innovation and collaboration across traditional boundaries.

This can lead to far more powerful learning and different engagement patterns throughout life. I see the world becoming a laboratory for thinking and doing, enabled by OERs and digitization. This is a very different perspective. OERs can put "learning by doing" on steroids. Only in this learning by doing, we will be able to focus on solving problems that are global but are largely invisible to the outside world even though billions of people are living with them. Problem-based learning solving real-world problems is the future."

▶ Gabriel Alba

"I'm a Panamanian student who has just graduated from the Civil Engineering Department at the National Taiwan University. This is the story of how I became acquainted with the Open Education Consortium and benefited from their resources.

It was not until the end of my senior year in high school that I knew of the existence of the Open Education Consortium and its Open Courseware. In June 2010, I was selected with three other students to represent Panama in the XV Latin American Physics Olympiad. While it was a huge honor to represent our country in such an important event, it was also a very daunting task. I remember that during the first meetings a professor mentioned how much *self-study* would determine our competitive advantage in this tournament, and that we would have to rely on *free online lessons* since the preparation time was short.

I must confess I was slightly clueless at the very beginning until one of the professor's assistants kindly guided us around this sea of available resources and helped us select courses according to our requests. I remember watching physics lectures from the top engineering schools, including the MIT Engineering School and the Stanford Engineering School. I was in awe of having the opportunity to learn from such renowned lecturers and receive top quality education for free, by taking their lessons offered that were crucial for our preparation. Little did I know that courses offered at the OEC would later become an important part of my college life.

After I graduated from high school, I decided to pursue an engineering degree at the National Taiwan University, which is mostly taught in Chinese. There were several times when, due to the language barrier and complexity of the lessons, I needed post-class reinforcement. In many occasions I turned to books and assistance from professors and classmates, yet these options were at times not so effective. I remember the first time the calculus teaching assistant returned our quizzes. I had the feeling that I did not perform quite well and my suspicions were confirmed as I grabbed mine and realized that I had failed.

As the teaching assistant handed my test to me he said: 'You should try practicing with online courses, it might help you.' Suddenly I remembered I had been ignoring a very powerful tool that could (with proven experience) help me improve my performance in the class. And it did. Not only did I start using the OEC available courses for my calculus classes, but also for the rest of my equally challenging courses such as statistics, engineering mathematics, computer programming and engineering materials, just to mention a few. These lessons were available 24/7 and very satisfactorily complemented my on-site studies.

I take pride in saying that I completed my undergraduate program within the regular four-year span, and the availability of courses at OEC played an important role in the successful attainment of my degree. I am very grateful to OEC for carrying forward this project and will contribute, either as a professional or as a student, to the endeavor of making high quality education and training available for everyone, everywhere—because as life-long learners, we must acknowledge that *education is an essential tool for individuals and society to solve the challenges of the present and seize the opportunities of the future.*"

SAYLOR ACADEMY

When I spoke with Devon Ritter at Saylor Academy, he discussed the need to be always improving the quality of their courses and the assessments that they build into successful course completion. But he then addressed a change in their focus based on the experience they have accumulated over the last several years.

"Historically, we have been open to let learners make whatever use of our resources they want. Currently, we are concentrating on how to focus our resources on specific external needs to be of greater service to learners. We are also considering selling institutional access to our learning platform.

That would combine our content with the other services that institutional partners have in play. For example, in some cases we are providing upper-level courses to learners who are nearing graduation but are also on the verge of dropping out. The University of Memphis is such a partner. There, over three hundred students have saved more than $400,000 using our courses to graduate. That's a great outcome."

Saylor's early years as a nonprofit were focused simply on opening up access to high quality learning opportunities that interested learners had previously missed out on, particularly for reasons of money, geography, or time. Saylor's asynchronous course model has proven to be particularly useful for individuals, many of whom are working adults who need the flexibility to learn on their own schedule.

While Saylor itself does not confer degrees based on the completion of these courses, they do partner with a number of institutions who will. Currently Saylor has relationships with 20 Transfer Partner Colleges and Universities and is a course contributor to the Alternative Credit Project™ (saylor.org/partner-schools/).

There is also the possibility to complete a large portion of a degree through the use of Saylor Academy courses, as evidenced by two existing degree programs created with Saylor's partner schools, the Open Course Option for ASBA offered at Thomas Edison State University and their partnership with City Vision University.

The Open Course Option for ASBA is then a new degree pathway because it allows students to complete the majority of an Associate in Science in Business Administration degree by taking free, open, online courses from the Saylor Academy that are aligned with the what Thomas Edison State University calls its prior learning assessment program. (tesu.edu/business/asba/Open-Course-Option.cfm)

Whereas the programs with TESU and City Vision were designed specifically for students who have had no previous college experience, Saylor is also working with schools to help with degree completion for those students who have already completed most of their required coursework. For instance, as a course provider option for the University of Memphis' Finish Line Program (memphis.edu/innovation/finishline/) mentioned above.

The Saylor Academy Corporate/Employer Degree Completion program aims to help students where they are: at work. Through the program, Saylor Academy works with employers to scale the impact of employee education benefits, such as tuition discounts, assistance, and reimbursement.

Saylor Academy works with employers in other ways as well. Beyond the benefit of an actual degree, many employers are recognizing the value of non-degree professional development and education, as a way to enhance soft skills and broaden their employees' knowledge base.

In addition to being one of the few free providers of recognized and transferable college education, Saylor Academy is also one of the pioneers in the growing field of Open Education. Saylor's commitment to openness proves valuable for both formal and informal learners. On the formal side, in addition to courses being used directly as a means of earning college credit, students use OER curated by Saylor to supplement or prepare for other educational opportunities. This use case can perhaps best be described using a student's own words:

"Three years ago, I finished my MBA and realized I wanted to further study economics, despite having taken only one economics class before and needing additional math courses. My advisor suggested I prioritize taking math classes and teach myself the economics before beginning my PhD program. I was able to catch up by taking economics courses through Saylor Academy.

I recently finished my first year and was in the minority of my classmates to have passed comprehensive exams on the first try. It was the most challenging year of my life, but rewarding to know that I had made it through with such an unconventional foundation. I owe a lot to the people of Saylor Academy for providing me with the resources to launch my education in this new direction. I honestly believe that I couldn't have made it here without all of your work. Thanks again."

On the more informal side, open courses created by Saylor Academy give students an opportunity to learn subjects that they may never have had the opportunity to learn. Whether that is STEM education for learners who previously focused on the liberal arts, or art history for those who have not previously had the opportunity to devote time or resources to the study of arts and humanities, the open practices employed by Saylor have helped to expand access to education, even if much of that learning has been undertaken simply for the love of learning and nothing more. (Paraphrased from Saylor Academy material.)

LOW-RESIDENCY PROGRAMS

Low-residency programs are not a new phenomenon. Pioneered in the 1960s by innovative institutions such as Antioch College and Goddard, low-residency programs provided a way for working adults to continue working and attend school intensively on weekends or during limited residencies two or three times a year.

Initially, these programs provided access by reframing the uses of time and space as well as the types of teaching and learning models that were employed replacing the lecture model then dominant in higher education. With the advent of technology and "free-range learning," however, the low-residency model has been put on steroids. One such example is the Vermont College of Fine Arts, a postbaccalaureate institution with master's programs in seven areas including music composition, art, film, writing, and graphics animation. (www.vcfa.edu)

In this model, which can be applied in multiple subject matter areas beyond the arts, learners attend two one-week intensive residencies each year where they work with advisors, subject matter expert faculty, and each other. All students are practicing in the field of their degree work, so the program of work at the college reinforces their artistic endeavors year-round.

Technology enhances the advising and coaching learners receive regularly between residencies as they work on their projects. Technology also provides "showcases" where work can be shared and "meeting rooms" where learners can connect with each other. And technology provides a platform for showing work once completed. This approach allows artists from all over the country and the world to be part of an academic and a creative community.

As VCFA president Tom Greene puts it,

"Low-residency education, which has been around since the early 1960s, has been transformed by technology. The largest transformation has been in the arts—namely the opportunity to educate students in fields that previously had been relegated to only residential education. Filmmakers now upload scenes onto Vimeo, a faculty member on the other side of the country reviews them, and the two get on Skype and together go through it frame by frame. Low-residency had always worked well for the written word, but an artist was not about to mail a painting. Vermont College of Fine Arts is fundamentally an experiment in community. Previously, the community, like residential programs, existed primarily within the bounds of our brick and ivy campus but just for two weeks a year. Now that experiment is ongoing and increasingly global."

THE ASSOCIATION OF EXPERIENTIAL EDUCATION

One other interesting resource for learners who want to learn as individuals is the Association of Experiential Learning (AEE). As Rob Smariga, AEE's CEO says, "Experiential learning is now a viable option throughout the life span in primary education, secondary education, gap years, service learning, higher education, mental health and therapy, and corporate training. Experiential learning, with its emphasis on novelty, feedback, and social engagement, is ideal for the adult learner."

AEE has created a web site (www.LearnThroughExperience. org) to help individuals find an experiential education program that best meets their needs.

The ecosystem supporting independent learning and connecting it to college, careers and life is a growing and thriving sector in the GPS for Learning and Work.

Whether you approach harnessing the value of your personal learning with a job and career in mind as your top priority or simply finding a friendly college to help you, these resources will put you in the driver's seat as you scout out your options.

Chapter 7, "Getting the Skills You Need," will sharpen your understanding of the new programs that are emerging to help you forge a direct connection between your learning and more satisfying and challenging work. The four services that I have given as examples are by no means the only players in this space. They are, however, known entities with proven track records of success.

Importantly, as you consider the larger implications of "A GPS for Learning and Work," remember that none of these entities could have existed ten years ago. Today they are thriving in a newly emerging ecosystem of learning and work preparation. There is much more to come.

7

GETTING THE SKILLS
YOU NEED

ANOTHER IMPORTANT PART OF THE disruptive change hitting colleges and employers is an emerging focus on more closely aligning job-related skills and abilities, wherever and however you got them, and actual job requirements. In the case of recent college graduates, for instance, employers are coming to recognize that often there is a significant gap between what is represented on a person's college transcript and their ability to work effectively in a given job. In short, while they may have been ready to graduate, they were not ready to work.

This situation calls for a closer alignment between college programs and actual work requirements. It also calls for employers to develop ways to better understand a person's readiness to work, wherever they gained the knowledge, skills, and behavior that they have. And this in turn opens the door wide to a better valuing of a person's hidden credentials.

You may remember the old yarn from the State of Maine in which a man in a hot air balloon lands in a farmer's pasture. He calls out, "Which way to East Vassalboro?" The farmer, leaning against his aging John Deere tractor replies, after considerable pondering, "You can't get there from here." It's a funny story about rural Maine. But when it comes to getting a job, it isn't funny at all. Because whatever your goal—to move up, get a new job, or get a first job—a combination of the traditional reliance on degrees, vague job descriptions, and a "we've always done it this way" attitude, often means you can't get "there" from where you are.

But good news is on the way. There are already several new programs that are designed precisely to help you analyze your strengths and weaknesses, define your immediate career objective, and prepare you for that reality without the sponsorship of a college. They are formally organized to connect directly with work, in most cases, and what you learn is aligned directly with jobs that exist and are available. This chapter provides descriptions of four such programs and the words of their leaders and users.

GENERAL ASSEMBLY

General Assembly (GA) is a global company, working in more than twenty markets around the world, including dozens of campuses across the United States. They focus on tailoring education precisely to technology-related jobs (data, design, tech, and business) that need to be filled, or to up-skilling people already employed by a company. They have a wide knowledge of the IT skills needed across employment sectors in manufacturing, financial services, health, transport, media, creative, and tech.

They also offer training packages to prepare students for the opportunity to pursue what they call a new kind of "hybrid job" that blends technology and marketing roles and requires a combination of programming skills and traditional business skills. General Assembly intends to fill the gaps for job seekers who have graduated from computer science programs or traditional vocational IT schools and have not been taught basic business skills as well as the design and business school graduates who enter the job market with little technical knowledge. And they also work with employers to assess and transform their current or in-coming talent. For more on this, check out: (www.burningglass.com/research/hybrid-jobs/).

They emphasize an "education to employment" approach in which learners self-select the kind of training they need. They call themselves "career accelerators," who enable you to acquire skills and improve your career trajectory through accelerated programs and services. For instance, for their students that are transitioning into a new field, General Assembly—unlike most colleges and many other training programs—tells you what the employment outcomes have been for previous graduates and what the diversity profile of the student body has been. Check out that report at www.general-assemb.ly/blog/general-assemblys-first-student-outcomes-report/.

Importantly, General Assembly offers a wide variety of learning modes so that you can find the learning path most appropriate for your needs and life realities. There are part-time programs, full-time programs (ten to twelve weeks), online courses, and in-person courses. Check out their course catalogue: at www.generalassemb.ly/browse/courses-and-classes.

Now let's meet some General Assembly learners.

▶ Christy Leung

"I am from a very traditional Chinese family. My parents gave me choices, and I chose from that list, initially. I chose accounting and finances. So I got a double bachelor degree in Accounting and Finance and went to work with banks and CPA firms.

Although this was a personal life direction choice, I was bored very quickly and began to feel the constraints of that career path. Therefore I began looking around. My fiancé was in programming because of the freedom involved. And I loved the creativity and the freedom. I thought to myself, programming can allow me to think creatively and change the world, but accounting cannot.

I wanted to learn as much as I could about this new vision I had. So, I started a website, pink TV, and I began to capture all the things I was viewing and resources I was accessing, including online tutorials. But, as great as the informality of it was, I was having a hard time getting answers to questions that got generated by my reading and viewing. And I needed answers and a course of action.

My fiancé's sister worked at a startup called SwitchUp (www.switchup.org) which contained reviews of different programming boot camps. I read them all, and that's how I initially learned about General Assembly. I talked with people in the boot camps, and after a while, I determined that the mode at General Assembly was more suited to my preferences.

They have a group style, whereas other boot camps did more individual work. You work in different combinations of people just like the real world. And I thought the curriculum and activities were more practical and job-related than academic. So 'how' we were asked to do things was part of the learning process.

The program lasted three months. In the beginning, I was very nervous and uncertain because I had already spent the money while the payoff was still far off. Was I meant to be doing this? Was the instructor sugarcoating the reality, and if and when I get a job would it be on my own? But, in fact, the curriculum included other services in addition to the daily learning. For example, the instructor helped us learn how to problem-solve on our own. And there were opportunities to learn more after class as well. The more you put in, the more you got out of it. Some people worked according to the norm, but if you wanted to do more, you could. They had anticipated these aspects as well.

At the end of the three months, I expected everyone would have something to show on the showcase. I wanted something to do with 3-D and VR, but I wanted to stand out, to be more than one of the crowd. During GA, I participated in the

'Angelhack' in Austin one weekend. More extra work. My team won the Angel Hack competition. Being able to prove that I could be part of a winning team even though I was coming from a non-tech background was amazing. I competed successfully against others who had graduated from a four-year program. This all resulted from the work that I did, and that GA supported, that was extra to the core program that I had signed up for.

After the showcase, I was getting interviews within two days. I got an offer within one week. But I waited until I received more because I wanted more than a job. I wanted the right fit between me and the company. They had also taught us about interviewing for jobs and, more deeply, how to think about your next step. What company, what direction?

I accepted a start-up job as a back-end node Java Script developer. I left the job recently, after only one year because I had a better opportunity both in pay and responsibility as well as size of the company. I am a front-end developer— things you see as opposed to what is inside the box and makes the box run.

Now, I feel like I am living the life that I wanted to live. I am not stuck with a dead-end job. I am working both back and front end. That is the biggest and best outcome benefitting myself and my life and my colleagues. I am still learning all the time. I am finding lessons and other skill improvement resources. GA gave me not only the knowledge, but also developed my problem-solving ability, and then they helped me develop as a conscious learner. Learning how to learn is a big piece of the learning."

▶ Jearold Hersey

"After high school I went through several colleges and jobs, including a stint in the army. I had been married and divorced and was a single father with responsibilities. I had worked at a lot of places, like Facebook and Apple, but nothing had worked out.

When I learned about General Assembly, here's the situation I was in: I had a job that I didn't like, had gotten divorced but had kids and couldn't go back to school the old-fashioned way, and trying to self-educate on top of a forty-hour work week wasn't happening. I decided to have a couple of interviews with them. They fit my needs in terms of accessibility and focus. Right about then, my employer let me go. That was fine with me because it was a bad fit both ways. I did the ten-week course in User Experience and Design, an immersive course from nine to five every day.

I wanted to get a handle on the new vocabulary and tools that I needed and the informal learning wasn't getting it done. There were folks there who were also making a mid-career shift, some from tech and some not, some in grad school and this was extra summer work. A very diverse set of reasons and aspirations.

I got exactly what I had expected. I had begun to learn some of the stuff on my own, but the GA experience really deepened my knowledge. We finished the ten weeks working with a real-world client and did that for the last three to four weeks. This meant there was classroom work with professor feedback coupled with the real-world experience of working on a real product.

They also emphasized networking and introduced us to employers. They hosted events as opportunities for us to learn more and get a job.

After the course, we were all a little nervous, like what is going to happen now? Finishing the portfolio was important because it portrays the work that I did at GA, getting it all tight and aligned. The job that I have now, I was introduced to the employer by one of my instructors. Razorfish came along in mid-December and that was it. I love the company. The uncertainty of being in a new field was a surprise even with the great experience at GA. When you are stepping into a role that you haven't done before, it is a totally new, as in first-time, experience. So, even though my diverse background was a strength during the Interview process, the future, in literal terms, was an unknown.

One of the advantages of coming at it later in life was that I had a whole lot of experience and job-based learned knowledge that gave me strength. I had more arrows in my quiver than I thought. It's not like I have to throw away a lot of my previous experience. There was a learning curve with my team, but I brought a lot with me as well.

At many of the jobs I've had since the Army, I've had a good five to six years of experience over many of the people I was working with. I was talking and working with people who didn't have a lot of real-world experience. The intelligence was there, but they hadn't had the chance to really apply it in real-world situations. They didn't know how to talk to their boss in a difficult situation, or how to handle it when a client is coming on too strong.

GA was the bridge to get me where I needed to go. UX Designer was the destination. I knew what I couldn't and didn't want to do educationally, but GA became the positive path. And it built on the learning and experience that I had already had and tied it all together.

Taking a risk is scary. When I was interviewing with no offers, it was tough. During tough times you see who really has your back. But when I got this job, the way people reacted was really wonderful. When you take a risk, you need help. And that is what GA does. They are making it more accessible."

Jearold gives a fine example that demonstrates how, if you are having a hard time finding a job and the skills to do it, and employers are having a hard finding people ready to work, General Assembly and other "boot camps" could be the bridge that you can walk across to a better job. And another great thing, as you will see in the next few examples, is that you can do it again and again to refresh and renew your skill sets and knowledge.

INNOVATE+EDUCATE

A national nonprofit based in Santa Fe, New Mexico, Innovate+Educate solves the problem of preparing you for and connecting you to the job you want from a different angle. Founder and CEO Jamai Blivin and Chief Technology Officer Steve Yadzinski told me the organization has a paradigm-shifting mission as they focus on multiple career centers that range from retail to health care, hospitality, and technology. Their goal is to work with local employers to clarify the competencies that underpin successful performance in each job and develop focused, competency-based training to prepare you for that job. And they believe that in the free-range learning era, they can find, assess, and further develop talent that would not surface using traditional hiring methods.

Imagine a job service that:

- matches you with available jobs, assessing your soft skills as well as your more traditional hard skills,
- helps you get the learning you need, when you need it,
- eliminates systemic bias against people like you in the hiring process, and
- encourages you to plan a career path going forward so that you can pursue your education based on a real understanding of what employers are looking for.

Innovate+Educate (I+E) is a program that links adults with better jobs either through up-skilling from the job they have or training for a new job that exists. I+E uses a process that has four steps: assess, train, hire, and advance. They also help you move up the ladder from your current job. Imagine a program that worked with you and your employer to make you upwardly mobile in your current company.

Steve Yadzinski puts it very bluntly, "The IT supporting learning and distribution will improve; price points a will come down. Virtual Reality applications will improve the quality and cost of delivery and the training itself. It is inevitable that employers will get better at listening to and acting on alternative indicators for quality preparation other than courses and degrees."
(www.innovate-educate.org/)

▶ *Darren Bradley*

In Dallas, Texas, for instance, Darren Bradley was an entry-level employee of the Dallas Area Rapid Transit Authority who received a raise and a promotion to supervisor II due to the Innovate-Educate process. Innovate+Educate, the Dallas Area Rapid Transit authority (DART) and Cedar Valley Community College took the guesswork and risk out of Darren Bradley's move up the ladder at DART. Listen to his story. (http://earndallas.org)

> "When I graduated from high school in 1981, I went to the local community college in Brooklyn, but dropped out after a semester and joined the Army. I didn't have any better choices and it seemed like a good thing to do. After four years, I left the Army, moved to Dallas to be with my brother and joined the Army Reserve in 1986. I had a couple of other jobs, but I got a job at DART as a driver in 1990 and have been there ever since.
>
> The years since then seem like a blur. I didn't want to go back to college. But the army reserve had courses I could take. Between 1986 and 2013, I was in the reserve, with another full-time stint in the Army from 2006-2010 sandwiched in the middle. I graduated from four courses in that period of time: Drill Sergeant, NCO Evaluation, and 1st and 2nd

Sergeant Major, and I became a supervisor 1 at DART along the way.

But then I was sorta stuck. My daughter was on her way to college, but I couldn't afford to pay for her and myself. And I really didn't want to go to college anyway, because at my age, what's it going to lead to? And that's when this deal dropped into my lap.

Here's the way it worked. Innovate+Educate (I+E), Cedar Valley Community College, and DART hooked up in a three-way deal. I+E created a curriculum that met the college's standards and also addressed DART's competency requirements for Supervisor II. DART paid for the six courses that I took over three semesters. And all I had to do was take the courses, address the competencies, and finish to get promoted and get the raise.

What was really great about the courses was that they addressed the realities of work life as a supervisor. Sure, there was some book-learning. But the exercises, evaluations, and projects were designed with an understanding that we weren't greenhorn kids right out of high school. We were adults with significant learning and work experience under our belts. The whole curriculum was like an integrated experience with work and supervising people.

And the best part was that I knew that if I did the work successfully, I would get a promotion and a raise and be on my way up the ladder again. No 'ifs, ands, or buts' about it. That was the best part.

And it was a good example for my kids as well. My eldest daughter has graduated from college and is on her way. The younger three are still at home. But they have my example and their sister's example to guide them. And I might go back and finish the Associate's at Cedar Valley. With my earlier college work and the eighteen credits from the Supervisor II courses, I am on my way. They gave me a plan, and I am thinking about it. But right now, I want to relax and enjoy my completion and my promotion."

Darren earned new skills and moved up the ladder. Other people learn entry-level skills and get a new job. But whatever route is taken, this approach is different from most traditional career preparation because it matches learners with job opportunities and guarantees that success in learning will lead to a better future and a new job.

Innovate+Educate's ability to bring the college and DART together and create a competency-based approach that gave both partners confidence that their standards were being met made the difference. The ability to fine-tune with data analytics and offer curriculum that aligned with both sets of needs is an element of learning in the digital age. And Darren is on a path to success with options of more school and more advancement if and when he chooses.

▶ *Jeff Burkhart*

Jeff, on the other hand, experienced Innovate + Educate from the perspective of being the Human Resources Officer at Kroger's in Dallas.

"When I was new in my role, a colleague had started a program to provide an opportunity for management team members to get a professional certificate—it is called the Retail Management Certificate (RMC). The goal was to start providing high level training for our leaders, to level the playing field between those who have college degrees and those who do not.

We have a lot of associates who came in at entry level and have grown in the system. The question is: How can we help them get a chance at getting better jobs? Unlike a lot of the other guys, Innovate+Educate is interested in entry-level workers; people who have missed out, for whatever reason, on traditional college opportunities.

These folks were not able, for whatever reason, to avail themselves of a formal education. But the truth is that there are many job descriptions that call for a degree even when they really don't need one for successful performance. We can get people to high-five and six-figure salaries without a college degree if we have the right information.

My company decided to partner with Innovate+Educate. The participants agreed to engage in a survey to determine where people were in terms of their skills development with regard to five core competencies. Those competencies are customer service, communications, adaptability, critical thinking, and drive for results. I am a huge believer in the development of soft skills, as it helps associates relieve or minimize anxiety caused by interacting with others and thus leads to higher retention, enhanced potential, and increased productivity. We don't do it in schools and we don't do it in traditional training and development. But Innovate+Educate has figured out how to do it in the workplace.

I think Innovate+Educate's vision, both humanly and professionally is first class. Their Core Score Assessment identifies people's strengths in the five competency areas. It is a customized assessment that addresses key areas for each individual. It is innovative and, as far as I can tell, one-of-a-kind.

These core competencies are the characteristics that are most present in people who are successful in retail management. They are rolling it out to individuals to up-skill them. The offer is this: We will place you using the competency scale, then do the program and employ a post-assessment to see what your growth is. They are looking at skills that make you more employable in any situation, see what you are capable of, and then target training and development to the needs of the individual. This is all possible because of data analytics. It provides job seekers with validated records and skills going forward.

The company that gets solid data analytics and applies them to hiring, up-skilling, and leadership selection and training will become the employer of choice in the community. It's a win for everyone involved: employer, employee, productivity, work place culture.

So instead of just looking at the traditional skills that a job requires, you are also looking at the individual's soft skills to get a better match. The job skills are specific to the job and the Core Score on soft skills is cross-cutting. I get the greatest impact when I am looking at entry candidates. The soft skills are more valuable. I can train for the job skills.

Can you assess soft skills? Yes. Can you train for them? Yes, but it is a lot more difficult. In lay terms, I say "hire for attitude, train for skill." I save myself a lot of time and money. Hiring and promoting with a focus on 'people skills' leads to greater longevity and higher potential for promotion. This allows for a path from entry to leadership training. Core Score will tell me who the higher performers are and whether they can take what they learned and apply it in other settings. When the score improves, it is evidence that they have improved their ability to apply soft skills in practice."

DEGREED

Kelly Palmer, the Chief Academic Officer of Degreed (www.degreed.com), described what their guiding vision has been from Day One as follows:

"Degreed was founded in 2012 by David Blake. Education had been a passion for David for many years. That passion stemmed from a negative personal experience. When he was preparing for college, David, along with millions of other high school seniors, took the SATs and ACTs to get into college. A good college and a good career were his goals. But, just like many other high school seniors, his scores were not as good as his record in high school, and his future was compromised in terms of work and learning opportunities.

He decided that he wanted to 'jailbreak education' and the degree, and that people should be able to get credit for skills in other ways. Degreed is a consumer-facing product, a new currency that does not use college credit in recognizing learning whenever and wherever it happens—such as learning that happens outside of, before, and after formal education.

From the beginning, anyone could go, sign up and start tracking their learning. In 2014, however, things changed dramatically. Several companies came to Degreed and asked, 'Hey, can we do this for our employees?' So we expanded our focus to include enterprises as well as consumers.

We are moving into an age of personalized learning. You start with what you already know and then create a context for future learning by setting goals and seeing a pathway.

The whole idea is to help people discover, track, and measure (build skills) for all the learning they are doing.

For discovery, we employ a massive amount of machine-curated content. The more you use it the better the results. It is highly personalized. In addition to discovering pieces of content, you can also view collections of content and create pathways. We have several hundred pathways already hand-curated and preplanned.

We also want to track all the learning you do, formally or informally, into a steadily-expanding lifelong learning profile. We have a mobile app and browser extensions where you can type in every podcast you do, for example, and then either mark it as complete or make a comment. Whatever you do, you then click on your browser extension, and it is stored immediately.

It is terrific to have all the learning on the record and in the profile. But there is another extremely important value to this. It puts you as the person remembering your learning in the center, the mainstream, of your learning activity. We want people to realize that they are learning all the time. Among other things, when you list some learning you have done, read an article, a podcast, you name it, we ask you to list your 'takeaways' and really internalize the learning.

And we are looking at measuring and recording the activities and evidence that you are moving up the skill and competence ladder. We started off as a consumer-facing product. But corporations are interested in what they can do for their employees. And there is a mind-set shift towards 'motivated learning' as opposed to 'dictated learning.' When we talk about measurement, the first part is to see what you are really learning, identify what you are doing and what skills you are building. Identifying what you know and then doing a gap analysis against your objective is the way the skill certificates work."

▶ Trisha Ward

Trisha Ward is a great example of someone who later in life developed the "habit" of curating and reflecting on her personal learning as a "usual and customary" part of her life. Supported by the curated learner profile supported by Degreed, Trisha is keeping track of her learning and making plans for more.

"I have always been a learner, and learning excites me. In fact if I am not involved in learning something, I am less happy. I first learned about Degreed from a webinar that I had clicked into. And I thought it was terrific. It looked intuitive and provided a great way to track and explore learning.

I am in corporate training and am constantly keeping up with new information about computers, platforms, and really anything online. As background, I have been interested and active in online learning for years. In the early days of online learning, like fifteen years ago, I got a certificate in online teaching and learning through CSU-East Bay. It was comprised of four courses focused on how to do online teaching and learning. All courses involved online discussion boards, posts, and immersion in the topic. What better way to learn and experience the topic than completely on the web?

Since then I've continued to enroll in and attend MOOCs and webinars to keep learning as the world of change unfolded around me. You could say that I am in a perpetual cycle of self-generated learning.

Degreed is terrific because, even with the no-cost, individual license, *it is a living history* of my learning. I love the social interaction, the sharing, and I love the 'learning paths recommendations.' They are guided when you want, but you can also do your own thing if you want to. As you mark things complete, you can comment on anything and add your key takeaways. It keeps track of everything: books, articles, videos, podcasts and any comments you make about what you learned. It's kind of an online library to help you keep track of what you have done and learned. Like, 'I know that I saw that information somewhere . . .' Degreed also allows you to 'save' items you find and reminds you to return and complete them. All this can be launched from a simple Chrome extension and pop-up window, making it an easy thing to remember any part of the workflow.

Every day I get a personalized email with links to articles recommended to me based on my history and interests. I also get to see what people who I'm following have been reading. And I often find interesting new content there. Degreed provides different curated pathways on a variety of topics, and if you follow certain pathways and complete them, you can get connections with new knowledge that you may need for future growth. You can also create your own pathways to jobs.

There is a skill certification process as well where you can do exercises, show examples of your work, be reviewed by peers, and get a certified record of your skill sets.

Degreed is, for me, a way to curate content and have evidence of all my learning and content for myself in one place. It is a record of my journey, and it keeps me up-to-date regarding my learning and change. It also refreshes my memory and impedes the forgetting process. And, it's a fun way to connect people you follow to great content that they might be interested in and missed . . . a quick search and a couple of clicks sends it right to them.

You can learn anything online these days, and it can be overwhelming at times. Also, it's amazing that most of this content is free. I took a UPenn class in Positive Psychology through Coursera recently and then entered it into the curation on my profile, personalized and customized at Degreed. A wonderful purpose is being served as it is. It sustains my mental fitness and chronicles a DIY path."

▶ Juli Weber

Juli Weber brings all the elements of free-range learning to her role as HR director at Purch, an international company. Juli is based out of the Ogden, Utah, office. She had never really thought about her, or others' personal and informal learning and its value. Then a set of circumstances and events at work led her to confront her own "learning discrimination." And that led to a difficult decision regarding whether or not to take a chance on Degreed, a new education solution, as opposed to a more conventional approach using a Learning Management System (LMS) as she sought to get the in-house professional development culture that she thought was best.

"I love Degreed. My educational background was such that Degreed forced a paradigm shift. My grandmother and mother went to college. My mother went back when she was forty to get a degree.

All my sisters and I went to college. I always knew that I was going to college, and that was very empowering. I was very pro-college but, as I was going to learn, in quite a narrow-minded way.

My husband didn't finish college. He is very smart, and he is very successful working at a job that doesn't require a college degree. He has been a wonderful provider for his family for twenty years. His example contradicts my earlier vision of what higher education should be. He helped me begin to understand that there are multiple paths to success and happiness and that we all learn in different ways. I've been in HR for over ten years. I returned to college after my kids were born, and I have two masters. Fine. That's the path that worked for me. But in reality, there are other paths that are just as good.

I joined Purch in 2015 as Learning Director. They wanted a fresh start and they asked me, at the onset, to look for an LMS and do a learning needs assessment. I thought 'easy peasy, I can do this.' My boss suggested that I check out Degreed. So I enrolled in a webinar where they were discussing results of a learning survey they had done. I was blown away by what the research revealed. Namely that people learn very important and sophisticated things informally. They learn all the time and in many different ways. I was blown away.

Then I put the same questions in my in-house learning needs assessment. And guess what? I found out the same thing! Going in, we believed that there wasn't any learning going on inside the organization because there weren't any formal programs. But the data was crystal clear and contradictory to our assumptions. Even without a formal program of staff development, our people were learning skills, behaviors, and talents that they needed all the time. It turned out that over 75 percent of my organization had learned something informally in the last week!

As a recent hire, I was faced with a challenging choice. Should I go with Degreed, track and record the informal learning that was going on, and then fill in the blanks as needed? Or should I choose a traditional LMS, look good personally, have a successful rollout, and then risk being outdated and behind the times in a few short years? Degreed was not an LMS and I questioned whether it would serve my employees in the way the leadership team expected.

Well, long story short, I went with Degreed, and we have never looked back. Over time, as they have matured, it has paralleled and informed our development in Purch. Over the last year, the developments have been really great. Managers are developing their own pathways, and people are sharing informally all the time. We learn all the time, and yet most of that learning isn't formal, in a classroom. It's organic and just in time for the learner. It's modern.

Now that we have all these digital tools for accessing information, sharing and storing that information, I think resumes may well go the way of the old LP's. When you are presenting yourself to your next employer, you might just send them your professional work profile (LinkedIn) and your learning profile (Degreed).

At Purch, we are doing workforce planning, and we are using Degreed skill plans. They include soft and hard skills as well as core competencies. Our employees can also pick the 'next' job they want and begin developing their own skills gaps to be ready for the next job opening. The learning is self-driven and not mandated. There are a lot of choices and freedom and therefore engagement and empowerment. Also, there are mentoring groups, people who have identified themselves with the skills that others are trying to develop, so they can connect with them and gain insights to their experiences, advice, and personal direction as they think about where they want to go and how to apply what they've learned.

I was listening to something just this morning about non-traditional education, and the speaker said something that just blew me away. He stated that we need to be transferring what we learn into action or application. It's no longer about what you know, because Google knows everything already. What's valuable is what you can do with the knowledge you gain. The fact is that when you learn in real time and apply what you have learned immediately, that is 100x more powerful than getting a high score on a test. Degreed supports that type of learning, and that is adding real value to our workforce."

CREDLY

When I spoke with Pat Leonard, Executive Advisor at Credly, I learned that they offer a very different kind of service. Credly (www.credly.com) offers no assessment service and no content. Instead, they are a "digital credential platform that empowers organizations and individuals to recognize, communicate, and track verified achievement. Organizations using Credly issue portable and secure digital credentials that recognize those earning them and yield actionable data and insights about how and where the credentials are being used." Using Credly, individuals can:

- Capture and convey skills accurately
- Own and carry credentials with them
- Navigate the job market with skills and competencies validated by third parties
- Advocate effectively for themselves
- Get discovered by employers looking for their skill sets

And employers can:

- Hire on the basis of targeted skills, including non-cognitive skills
- Build better teams
- Engage and retain employees better with a culture of achievement and recognition
- Understand human capital better

Once you have your digital credential, you can take this granular description of what you've done, what you know, and the credential wherever you want.

▶ *Brenda Perea*

Brenda Perea was an educator with a problem. And she was looking for a solution that was not the "same old, same old" to solve some major problems that the State of Colorado was having matching people with jobs.

> "I have been in postsecondary education for at least eighteen years, most recently at the Colorado Community College System (CCCS). My job was to assist in the implementation of a grant to train workers who had been caught in the economic downturn. One of my strengths coming into this work was the ability to use open resources—Merlot, Rice, Open badges, and Mozilla to meet the terms of the grant. In 2013, during my first year helping colleges create and deliver open educational resources, Gov. Hickenlooper identified 15,000 unfilled jobs in advanced manufacturing which were impacting Colorado's economy, and he identified micro-credentials as a way to get people trained for those jobs.
>
> So in the Fall of 2013, I pulled together a taskforce of representatives from across the thirteen colleges within the system to develop an approach to digital badging which included

participating in industry specific sector summits to listen to employers detail skills gaps our manufacturing programs and credentials were not meeting.

At one of the earliest meetings, manufacturers stated CCCS advanced manufacturing graduates couldn't do the math required on the job. To meet this immediate need, I created a MOOC to address that issue directly and explicitly contextualizing math concepts in six topics: basic math, algebra, geometry, trigonometry, finance, and statistics. We ran the MOOC for ten quarters and served about 4100 learners.

In the last year, something interesting happened. We introduced twenty-three badges as a recognition for successful completion of specific sub-topics in the six topics, and there was an uptick in completion. The learners knew that they would get a badge if they completed a randomized twenty-five question test at 85 percent or higher on the first try. The MOOC course was developed using game-based theory, and with the introduction of digital badges, participants were successful in learning the math concepts in relation to advanced manufacturing.

As time passed, I noticed that there were more students coming from the employers, not just from the community colleges. The employers were sending their employees to the MOOCs to learn very discrete math skills need for performing their jobs, and the course work connected to the badging was working to enhance success. Today, Colorado Community College System has launched approximately 72 different badges—we have gotten over 91,000 social media hits on 536 issued badges, (see the badges on Credly.com.)

When developing digital badges, an institution cannot do it in a vacuum. At CCCS, we were not only interested in developing and issuing badges, but also building the ecosystem that the badges would live in as well. Acceptance of badges as a valid and verified credential depends on widespread knowledge of the metadata behind the badge, how they are issued, and the value of the competencies behind the badge. Badges have to fit into the existing credential framework that employers understand so that when an applicant or employee comes to them with a badge, employers understand the badge as a credential, trust it, and know what to do with it.

Historically, colleges have been very good at telling employers what we do, and presenting them with the program or credential we have developed internally and pushing out to the community. But we have been very poor at hearing what they need from the outside and building it internally. And the learners have gotten caught in the crunch.

Here's where Credly's approach is really cool. Credly sets itself apart from just providing a badging platform. They help the badge issuer understand how the badge will work in a course or program and assists them in considering how their product works in the open marketplace.

Hard questions are asked: Have you vetted this badge in the employer space? Do you know of any industry standards which apply to the badge? Will the badge work in a career or educational pathway? Service providers don't have to do that. But Credly does, and it leads to a far better service and helps the issuer make a better decision about the credential itself.

Credly's customers are a diverse lot: colleges, community groups, and employers. There is a focus on a Quality Assurance approach to the design and implementation of training and micro-credentials that are appropriately focused and validated with employers and industry standards. They bring transparency to the learning using a badge that reveals learning, knowledge and the application of the skills. Credly badges make skill sets and learning apparent to whomever views or consumes the badge.

I believe we are entering into the era of unbundling postsecondary education. Individuals are demanding multiple paths with multiple entry and exit points along an educational and career pathway. Credly allows the learner to create their own pathway with confidence about QA and transparency from a wide variety of institutions. It empowers the learner to showcase those credentials in a meaningful way. Credly maintains the metadata which validates and verifies the badge and their platform allows the portability and transferability of badges, keeping the metadata intact so wherever the badge sits, the information contained in the badge is verified and validated.

When an employer views a badge, they can use the URL to click through to the original issuer, view the issue date, competencies, and any other information relevant to the badge. What makes this possible is Credly's badges are built utilizing the Open Badge Standard code now supported by the IMS Global Learning Consortium. IMS Global is a nonprofit consortium focused on inter-operability standards. The Open Badge code allows for the rich metadata in badges to be portable.

Unlike most Learning Management Systems and internet services, Credly does not own the badge; the learner owns their own information. Therefore the control for the learning has been liberated."

In the GPS for learning and work that is coming soon, organizations like General Assembly, Innovate+Educate, Degreed, and Credly will be right there to connect learners with the jobs they want.

8

NEW TOOLS FOR THE NEW WORLD OF LEARNING AND WORK

THERE ARE MANY NEW TOOLS and services being offered in the developing ecosystem of learning and work. Collectively, as they are tested, validated, and organized, they will make up the "GPS for Learning and Work." This chapter describes several of these new services to give you a taste of things to come, as well as a sampling of what is already out there waiting for you to go and get it.

It is important to note that some of these services are available through colleges and universities, some are free-standing, and some may well become both over time. Successful innovations such as these will support free-range learning. They will also serve as markers of institutions which are serious about serving learners in the new ecosystem.

HelioCampus

For example, the University of Maryland University College (UMUC) began HelioCampus (www.HelioCampus.com) as its internal analytics function several years ago. As Michael Roark, CEO of Ventures/UMUC tells it,

> "As Helio's data science, visualization, and storytelling capabilities provided value to our students and administrators, UMUC's leadership spun off the team into a stand-alone company in 2016. Helio creates customized implementations to link together student data from across the institution — from marketing and admissions through student life and academics to graduation status and alumni giving. Once the student lifecycle data is in a unified system, University teams and their dedicated Helio data scientist discover patterns and opportunities. Helio believes that improvements are usually found in several areas with increasing student enrollment and improving student success leading the way."

The following are several examples of tools universities use to improve their provision of services to their students.

PORTFOLIUM – *Barbara Lomonaco*

Barbara is the Vice President of Student Affairs at Salve-Regina University in Newport, Rhode Island. As a small, private nonprofit university, Salve-Regina was struggling with the critical issue of improving and being able to document the connection between their undergraduate experience and their graduates being ready to work. They need this improvement to deepen their reputation as a university and to continue to build enrollments in a very competitive marketplace. Listen to her thoughts about the experience they have had with Portfolium and what they have learned. (www. portfolium.com)

> "I have spent my entire career as a faculty member and administrator at small, private colleges. Students and their parents have, since the financial crisis of 2008, begun to

push hard on questions such as 'What is the ROI on a college education? What jobs does your program prepare me for? How am I being prepared for life in the civic community?' In a nutshell, all of a sudden, small private colleges were being pressured to show their ability to produce career readiness.

There are many faculty members who still think career readiness is a tawdry topic, and that it cheapens the liberal arts experience. They don't know what career readiness is or what it means. But I am an applied anthropologist and have years of experience at demonstrating the application of a social science. So I am used to asking the question, 'How does your discipline apply to the real world?'

The challenge we are addressing deals with that question. How can we orient liberal arts and professional programs to career readiness? And how can we equip students with competencies and skills that enhance their learning and prepare them for the world of work? We use a developmental approach at Salve Regina in which programming is matched to the psychosocial needs of each student cohort. We sometimes call this the 'Russian nesting dolls' approach for these reasons:

- In the first year, students work on understanding their strengths and identifying their passions and values.
- in the second year, programming is focused on working collaboratively in a group.
- the third year focuses on community and civic engagement.
- the fourth year cultivates global citizenship and engagement.

By stitching the developmental work throughout the student's experience, we think it will have significant impact in the area of employability.

Another of the things we haven't done well at all historically is help students develop the vernacular for discussing with others, including employers, what they really know and can do as a result of their learning. And that's where Portfolium comes in. It is a terrific way to develop the vernacular that they need. Portfolium's structure and content is giving us a short-hand for mapping learners' undergraduate experiences, curricular as well as throughout student life, to larger human qualities and capabilities.

Reflection is an essential and mandatory part of the Portfolium experience. You don't just upload a picture or a video, or make a claim that you did something. You have to reflect on what you have done, describe what it meant to you, how you changed as a result. The reflective piece is a great feature of Portfolium. You can upload actual papers and other evidence. You must use evidence to substantiate each claim you make.

Portfolium is a tool that will help students get very clear about what they learned while developing the ability to showcase their talents and their strengths to the larger world. It connects learning with skills and competencies.

And the social media component is important for moving this information all over the place. As you can imagine, it is big with millennials. There is a profile and a portfolio and you can share them, like them, electronically. Coincidentally, employers can browse your website and search for students in particular programs as part of their search process as well. As a result, Portfolium's social media component creates a town square-like gathering space where learners and employers with similar interests can communicate.

In this way there is a very functional face value to Portfolium. It is a collection point for information that references all your learning to work readiness.

But there is a huge educational value to it as well. In order to use Portfolium, you have to reflect and extract the meaning from the experiences you have had. Meaning making is the deeper pedagogical value of this tool lying behind the face function. It becomes a great multi-dimensional digital showcase of the work and the learning I have done that also projects my skills into the work that life."

The great value that a service like Portfolium's provides is that it removes many of the unstated assumptions and guesswork that currently plague the college curriculum workforce-readiness environment. Instead of simply asserting that you are ready for work, Portfolium helps you develop and document the evidence that makes that critical link. As Barbara also points out, it is also deeply educational given its focus on the learner's reflection, which she calls "essential and mandatory."

COOL – *Lisa Lutz*

Lisa Lutz leads the team at Solutions for Information Design that is working with the different military service branches to develop the COOL platform. When I asked her to describe the point of COOL, she replied,

> "The Joint Services Credentialing Work Group (JCOOL) includes all the armed services. The main service they offer is focused on maximizing the value of credentials earned in the military by linking service credentials to civilian occupational credentials. That way, a service member leaving the service can search for close 'matches' between the training and experience they have had in the service and the civilian jobs that lie ahead in their lives.
>
> We use O*Net (www.o*net.gov), the Department of Labor data base of job skills, to link military training, experience, and credentials to civilian jobs. Our focus is on the civilian credential and bridging the military education with the credential using O*Net.
>
> COOL does the following things to execute on its purpose:

- Provides background information on civilian credentialing
- Identifies licenses and certifications relevant to military occupations
- Identifies detailed credential requirements and exam preparation resources
- Identifies gaps between military training and experience and civilian credentialing requirements
- Provides information on resources available to service members to fill gaps and facilitate credentialing
- Provides information to external stakeholders on the credentialing of service members and veterans." (Excerpted from "Overview of Services' COOL Programs," SOLID, LLC. 9/22/17)

The takeaway here for the returning service member is parallel to that of any other adult with personal learning and credentials that lie outside of the traditional college sphere. Now there is a way to get down to brass tacks, to identify the connections between what you know and the jobs for which your knowledge qualifies you; and identify the next steps to get you where you want to go."

- Army COOL (www.cool.army.mil)
- Department of Navy (DON) COOL (www.cool.navy.mil)
- Marine Corps COOL (www.cool.navy.mil/usmc)
- Air Force COOL (www.afvec.langley.af.mil/afvec/Public/COOL/Default.aspx)

CLIFTON StrengthsFinder® – *Brandon Busteed*

"One of the major complaints from employers has been that college graduates, or anyone coming to work for that matter, are not ready to be successful on Day One. One of the key facets of this lack of readiness is that they lack the "soft skills" that make you successful at work. And one of the reasons for this shortfall is that, while colleges may be very good at pre-testing and preparing and delivering courses to enhance learners' skills and experiences, they have not focused until very recently on talent and behavior.

In fact, as you look out at the landscape in the current discussion regarding higher education and jobs, the skills gap, and related issues, you see two predominant ways that people have been sorting things out—the individual's skills and experience. That's fine. But at Gallup Strengths Center® we argue that a complete education is really a three-legged stool. And the third leg to that stool is talent. We believe that talent, at this point in time, is significantly under-attended in the higher education and career-preparation world. We define talent as 'constantly recurring thoughts, emotions, and behaviors that can be practically applied.' For example, you could call a 'strong desire and tendency to always go up to new people and talk to them' as a behavior. And we would say that if it can be practically applied (sales people at a convention), then it's a talent.

StrengthsFinder is the source of information for defining and interpreting a person's talent profile. Talent is what you are born with. It is innate and it structures the way that you interact with information and the world around you. But you can lose your talent and its value to you. A lot of people who never use their talent lose that talent.

At the same time, people who are very successful in life almost always are harnessing their talent as well as their skills and experiences. Talent is the differentiator. And in a world where personalized education will become the norm, we can and should add the lens of talent to the outcomes we establish for learning and performance, be they academic or job-specific.

StrengthsFinder won't tell you what course to take or what job to do. It is not a jobs inventory or predictor. It does, however, give you a blueprint for how you can be successful in any work role by harnessing your strong traits. When it comes to educational situations, the same principle applies:

- If a person has an empathetic and caring behavior, what we would call 'a relator,' she might be better in group-learning situations, while someone who is competitive would do better going it alone.
- Asking someone who is a strategic thinker about their future to apply the same skills of critical thinking to the academic subject areas of history or literature might be a great idea.

The point here is that, as a teacher (or a learner), you can adapt the teaching mode to learner talent profiles and behaviors in the context learners are experiencing.

The real value-add that comes with StrengthsFinder is when the information is interpreted for the individual or the advisor/teacher by a trained coach. Somewhere around 25 percent of college freshmen are exposed to StrengthsFinder. The good news is their exposure. The "bad" news is we don't know what is happening as a result.

Since StrengthsFinder is a developmental tool, coaching strengthens its impact in most cases. We are training coaches to interpret strengths in school, college, and work. As we do that, however, it raises this question. 'To what degree are there learning infrastructures and uses which tie the information productively to personalized learning and work?'

Since the coaching can be real or virtual, it can also be personalized to the learner's situation in a DYI or an applied situation. And you can do the same with curriculum that is designed with behaviors and talent in mind as important outcomes with regard to the projects that learners are asked to do." (www.gallupstrengthscenter.com)

BURNING GLASS – *Matt Sigelman*

Burning Glass Technologies has developed and continually deepens its comprehensive data base of job-related skills. They work both with third parties as well as individuals to strengthen their work readiness.

"Our data right now deals with two directions: demand and supply. We have been able to distill them down to a consistent vocabulary. Skills are the genetic code of a job. You can then look for similarity and diversity within and among jobs. That in turn lets you create paths that can meet needs.

We have an engine which can break both jobs and resumes down into skills. It is a short leap to then tag learning bits to fill the gaps. So, you can not only write a prescription, but you have a content dispensary to draw on to fill the gaps as well.

We are also creating an analytic which identifies which skills are foundational for a job and those that are distinguishing. For example, a practicing psychologist makes in the low 40s. And, if someone decided to supplement their skills and become a marketing psychologist, they might enjoy it, but they would only make in the high 30s. But a psychologist with coding expertise will make a salary in the 60s. That's important information to have when you are thinking about a career path.

Also, there is another kind of diversification going on in the "broadening proposition" that I just described. Skill sets are becoming hybridized. So skills that traditionally had no business in an occupation, are now showing up. For example, a marketing manager who can build a data base using SEQUEL skills would be very valuable today, where ten years ago that would have been a nonstarter.

Therefore, having all this information in hand then lets you create learning paths that can meet learning needs that are specific to the person doing the learning. When you are writing a prescription for learning, a skill gap is a learning gap. So if you can identify the gap vis-à-vis a given job, then you can fill it with a learning plan." (www.burningglass.com)

FULL MEASURE EDUCATION (FME) – *Chuck Brodsky*

Full Measure Education has set their sights high. They want nothing less than a user experience in higher education and lifelong learning that is on a par with Amazon or NetFlix when it comes to personalized service. They envision a communications strategy that, using data analytics, anticipates your needs and facilitates your progress in every way possible. Chuck Brodsky, cofounder of FME, described how they can adapt the service to an institutional partner and are working to make it more generally available to the public through the Department of Labor:

> "There are two or three basic elements to our vision. The first is 'personalization.' If I had to boil our vision down to one word, that would be it, 'personalization.' The most important thing to focus on is personalizing the experience for the learner.
>
> Currently, there is a huge communications divide. In the real world, people are using smart phones to access and use information in ways that were previously unimaginable. There is a massive amount of information out there, and companies are personalizing it for you. Think about Uber. They don't own cars. But with the touch of a button you can get the ride you need. AirBnB is doing the same thing. They don't own property, but they get you where you want to be with the touch of a button.
>
> But higher education and lifelong learning services are still largely living in a world where learners (users/customers) are still expected to 'persist,' to endure and survive the process. So you have high expectations for personalization walk-

ing through the door and outdated, old systems and processes on the inside that cannot possibly meet those expectations. That is a recipe for failure.

At FME, we aim to make the process and the experience more adaptive and personal, from 'A' to 'Z.' We know that more people leave higher education without completing programs for administrative than academic reasons. There are hurdles and barriers everywhere, not because the information isn't there, but because it is everywhere, unorganized, and not personalized. We believe that personalization and simplification of the learner experience, closing the personalization gap, will do more to improve success in higher education and lifelong learning programs than any other strategy.

That leads to the second element. We operate on the belief that all the information that one needs already exists. The problem is that we lack the ability to access it usefully when it comes to higher education and lifelong learning. For example, there are a combination of steps that constitute the procedure for graduating from college: take the right courses, complete the forms, apply, and so on. We are working with a college that had large numbers of students who were qualified to graduate but did not because they got tripped up by all the steps they had to take, got frustrated, and walked away.

We analyzed the business work flow around what people had to do to graduate. That included identifying who the target students are, what they needed to actually do, and the necessary behaviors to do those things. Then we created a communications strategy that helped the college increase their graduation rate by 44 percent. This is business process simplification pure and simple. In higher education, there are hundreds of examples where you can create a communications plan and strategy that dramatically improves the learner experience.

And the third is that we want to move from assessing and characterizing symptoms of students who are headed for trouble to creating information strategies that help the student in the moment and looking forward.

Through our platform, you can connect student behavior with Google analytics and connect it to outcomes. At Brazo Sport Community College, for instance, we identified sixteen activities they were asking students to do as they entered college. The core purpose of the sixteen activities, collectively, was to get information that got them admitted, enrolled in the right program, and on their way.

We developed a communications plan to get all these things done in an integrated and user-friendly manner. In a trial sample, students who used the strategy enrolled at more than twice the rate of those who did not. By analyzing student behavior data, we empower students to be partners in, co-owners of, their life as a student.

So as we approach any problem these three elements— personalization, organizing abundant information, and a focus on prevention—are the lenses we use.

We can also do the same type of thing outside of the higher education world. We are working with the Department of Labor to transform the experience of people who are claiming unemployment insurance. We will then move to under-employed people and eventually to the general public.

The concept is to create a national platform that helps people determine what they can be good at doing, where the job is, and what they need to know to qualify. The platform will connect users to programs, courses, jobs, and other information that closes the gap and gets them where they want to go. This can happen for an individual throughout their life, not simply as a one-off.

If NetFlix can anticipate what you will want to watch next, and Amazon can successfully recommend your next purchase 30 percent of the time, and a mapping system can tell you the fastest way to your destination, why can't we do the same thing for personalized education and training through-

out your life? Our ultimate goal is integrated case management that brings all information to bear on the individual's
personal needs and situation."
(www.fullmeasureed.com)

What each of these services does in its own way is personalize
the experience you are having educationally. For example, with
Portfolium you are directly and intensively involved in building
your learning profile throughout your college years. Or with Burning Glass and Full Measure Ed, you can get the gap analysis and
begin to lay out a personal learning path. And, while Strengths-
Finder helps you identify that critical "third leg" of the "three-
legged stool to success" in career readiness as far as discovering
your talents, COOL will help you map your military training and
education to civilian job opportunities.

Each of these services puts the learner in the driver's seat, in
control of maximizing the value of your personal learning and
your hidden credentials. And they challenge the unspoken tyr-
anny of learning discrimination by employers and colleges that
has compromised and undercut the value of your personal learning over the years. As you consider programs and colleges for further learning, ask whether they employ support services such as
Portfolium or BurningGlass data to illuminate employment requirements. Colleges that use programs such as these are, in my
opinion, more likely to have your personal interests, needs, and
goals front and center.

Behind services such as those that have been described in section three, as with those colleges described earlier that are adult-
friendly, there are men and women of courage and vision who are
seeking a future that is different and better than the present-day
situation. Chapter 9 features the vision of six such leaders who are,
individually and collectively, defining the emerging ecosystem
and, with it, the "New GPS for Learning and Work."

9

THE INNOVATORS SPEAK

VISIONS OF A NEW WORLD
FOR LEARNING AND WORK

Much of the chapter text of *Free-Range Learning* has been in the words of adult learners, the users of both higher education and career preparation services. Just as we heard from selected college presidents, however, and asked them to describe what they believe tomorrow's learners require and deserve for success, I wanted to ask some of the leading educational entrepreneurs and innovators on the "business" side to do the same thing. In this case, however, I asked these leaders to describe what they think the future holds in terms of the continued disruption of the higher education and career preparation workspace.

Each of these people have significantly different views and ventures that they are developing. But there is a surprisingly consistent agreement on the important drivers and characteristics of this "new world of learning and work" that extends throughout much of their vision for their specific businesses as well as for the future.

First, and most obviously, comes the continued dynamic development of what we have previously called the "information revolution." The names of this movement may evolve, but there is no doubt that the ever-growing ubiquity of information and its uses through technology will inform all future visions.

This characteristic drives, in the eyes of the entrepreneurs, the ever-more precise use of data and data analytics to improve and personalize all aspects of the learning/work continuum. The leaders say we will see analytics that tie curriculum and assessed knowledge and abilities directly to assessed job readiness and actual job requirements. All types of skills and behaviors will be in lifelong portfolios of learning. And the actual learning that people do will be dynamic, life-long, and personalized.

This, in turn, presages a dramatically changed marketplace as predicted by Burck Smith in his comments below. As the business of higher education related to career preparation continues to develop and diversify, it will affect the following:

- The structure of academic programs
- Our understanding and consumption of the time needed for appropriate learning
- The ways we screen and admit candidates to programs
- The ways that we structure and employ content to promote better, more complete, and higher-quality learning
- The cost of the unbundled enterprise, both on a per-unit basis as well as collectively

As you read through these visionary interviews, you will see these characteristics surfacing again and again. Having a deeper understanding of and appreciation for these characteristics will help you be a smarter learner and consumer of "free-range learning" in our time.

▶ *Burck Smith*, StraighterLine

For Burck, the future is about an emerging marketplace in which technology puts tremendous and steadily increasing pressure on traditional pricing mechanisms.

"Technology, by its very nature, is supposed to lower prices, change business models, and reorder market participants. Just consider the examples of electric looms in the 1800s, automobiles in the 1900s, and the internet in the 2000s. That's the reason that new technologies are brought to market by companies and adopted by consumers. Except, so far, in education. My background is in public policy. So when I started StraighterLine, my proverbial hammer was the way that government regulations and subsidies structure markets, and the proverbial nail was the ever-rising price of higher education despite the presence and adoption of much cheaper new technologies.

When I read *The Innovator's Dilemma* by Christensen, I began to think about how the theory of disruption applied to colleges. The pricing mechanism in postsecondary education is dysfunctional in the extreme. Money comes from multiple sources—grants, appropriations, endowments, subsidized interest, tax credits, financial aid, tuition, and fees—among others. And costs are variable and affected by multiple drivers such as length of time to get the degree, assessment of prior learning, credits transferred, type of institution, textbooks used, annual appropriation increases, and so on.

Effectively, there is no functioning pricing mechanism in higher education that lets consumers respond to lower prices. This market dysfunction is maintained because vast taxpayer subsidies flow to colleges using accreditation as the gateway. This combination of subsidization for a particular business and organizational model makes it very difficult for new models that offer lower prices to compete. Therefore, the market can't adapt.

In essence, the productivity benefits of online learning are being captured by colleges (and online program management providers) rather than being passed on to students in the form of lower prices. This creates the central tension in online college programs.

On the one hand, colleges are not interested in creating low-cost pathways into themselves, nor should we expect them to be. Colleges want students to take their courses at their prices with their profit margins. On the other hand, colleges want transfer students and are willing to award credit to attract them.

As colleges have come under greater competitive pressure from each other and political pressure from policymakers, more and more are willing to take credits from nontraditional sources to better attract and keep students. Interestingly, this approach to market change deliberately ignores the elite and flagship colleges who, by definition, have more student demand than they can fulfill. Not surprisingly, these colleges are the most resistant to making a degree more affordable. They also represent a small minority of today's college students.

In 2009 Kevin Carey wrote an article for the *Washington Monthly* called 'College for $99?' which thrust StraighterLine into the spotlight where it remained as a lightning rod for disruption until the MOOC moment in 2012. Between then and now we've steadily grown. We have a partner college base of over 130 colleges with students reporting credit being transferred to nearly 2,000 other colleges. We enrolled about 22,000 students in the last twelve months and about 75,000 in total. Most recently, we were accepted into the DOE's EQUIP program, which lets colleges outsource up to 100 percent of a program to nontraditional providers. We believe this will lead to low-priced OPM programs as opposed to the current batch of high-priced OPM programs.

When economics and fairness meet is when disruption begins to go mainstream. But the regulation and subsidization of higher education create barriers to transformative low-cost, high quality services.

Here are some other core elements of StraighterLine's proposition:

- About 62 percent of students successfully complete at least one course. As important, most unsuccessful students stop within the first month which greatly reduces their financial risk relative to enrolling directly in college.
- We offer a free trial followed by a month-by-month subscription to reduce failure and loss of money by the students.

Attitudes have changed dramatically toward online learning and out-sourced learning since the MOOCs burst on the scene in 2012. When the elites began entering the market, the status issues faded. More importantly, it validated the model that we'd built and highlighted our commitment to quality course delivery. For instance, we required online proctoring for all courses starting in 2012, which is something that many colleges still don't do. Our assessments are psychometrically valid and reliable, which is a higher level of assessment than is currently provided elsewhere. Students are given up to ten hours of live, online tutoring as part of their enrollment. E-textbooks are bundled into the price rather than a required fee. We have live academic advisors available for student up to twelve hours per day.

The market is changing more slowly than many of us would like. But it is changing. And I am very pleased and proud to have been one of the drivers bringing fairness, low prices, and quality together in service to America's learners."

▶ *Jonathan Finkelstein,* Credly

Jonathan Finkelstein, CEO of Credly, started with a vision of the services he wanted to provide and how they would improve learners and users lives.

"In the beginning, we had a grand vision. We wanted to bring *all* the capabilities that people have, however and wherever they were gained, to the forefront. Many skills and behaviors have historically been ignored in the documentation of knowledge. And to compound the problem, individuals, colleges, and employers all use different languages, different documentation systems, and different processes to describe skills when they operate in this space. So individuals write resumes, employers use generalized job descriptions, and colleges use transcripts. None of the three align with the others.

Our questions included:

- How can we align individuals, employers, and colleges and their needs?
- How can we convert data and analytics into information that is useful to all three?
- How do we provide a tool that verifies skills and competencies in a language that all understand and trust whether claiming them or looking for them?

Our partners and customers, the users of credentials, are educational institutions, training providers, trade and professional associations, and employers. In other words, anyone who provides education/training and wants to communicate the qualifications of their students, members, or employees.

Our *consumer* of a credential is the individual who earns this form of recognition. Importantly, however, our *audience* is the party looking to understand those qualifications earned, whether for the purposes of assessing a job applicant, mapping a career pathway, confirming expertise, or satisfying a requirement (among other things).

We have created a platform where people can author and create standards for qualifications. They can create competency profiles to which people can continually add and update. They can also issue validated credentials and manage badges.

The learners, our users, use the updated and verified evidence in their personal profiles which contain verified skills and credentials. The Credly Profile is a modern transcript, the container of all pertinent learning information. It has within it smaller, more basic 'containers 'of information, each specific credential or badge including the description of skills, criteria met, evidence attached, and all other pertinent validating information.

When we started, we had this feeling that the great value of a portable credential and profile is just that, its very portability. So we are not aiming for a narrow niche or specific sector. Our vision is for the service to be lifelong and to extend across involved sectors of education and training, professional associations, and employers. The goal is to let users identify and use pathways within each and among all three sectors. For employers, for example, understanding the talent you have on hand is critical.

With all this in mind, we have been focused on the teaching and assessment of skills and abilities from the beginning, working with third parties to scale learning in new ways and cultivate new experts in new ways. The question quickly became 'How do I get value and recognition for what I have learned?' From this we understood immediately that there was a huge need to get a new tool and new currency that not only recognizes the learning, but also explains the learning to the satisfaction of the ultimate audience.

The goal is to make sure that people can take their learning and skills profiles with them for use anywhere and anytime. The key here is the use of data analytics that match credentials and jobs in detail and make far better comparisons so that both the user and the employer know where they stand. This can include a gap analysis indicating the need for further learning, as well as other jobs that are within the users reach using the same cluster of skills.

There are a number of consequences generated by our service that, while not intended, are important and valuable to note. First, there is what we call the emergence of a 'culture of recognition'—a different mindset for the learner. Users report a sense of empowerment because they have greater control over their career and professional development. With consistent descriptions of skills and jobs, within and between businesses, the user is far more empowered to access jobs otherwise invisible to them. And college presidents are reporting that their students are far more articulate about the details of their learning.

One of the concerns we hear from people when we talk about micro-credentials and new types of credentials, is 'How do we make sense of this going forward?' We believe this is a data problem that technology can solve. The next stage is that we get better at the bits of knowledge and skills that lie within with a course, or an assignment. Then we can develop information that always existed but was never harvested.

The bottom line is that we not only harvest evidence of learning but also help users analyze their more concrete skills and knowledge while helping employers understand more deeply what bundle of knowledge, behavior and skills they are really looking for. The underlying assumption here is that we want to transition from simply using the user's profile as a snapshot of the current state to using the profile as a basis for projecting future opportunities and pathways."

▶ *Anant Agarwal*, edX

Anant Agarwal, CEO of edX, has an expansive view of the future, informed by his years of experience at edX. He is excited about the future.

"Where will things be in five to ten years? Well, the walls are coming down and the direction in which we are we are going is modular education enabled by a process of unbundling. Today we know the process: testing and admissions, enter, go up the ladder, get all your services from the university. Also, you are laser programmed towards the degree you choose.

But the degree will be unbundled. I see a world unfolding where everything will become modular and blended—not in four-year and two-year chunks, as it is today, but in modular components like the MicroMasters programs. With Micro-Masters programs today, the master's degree credential is unbundled, so you can earn a piece of a master's and get a job, or you can stack MicroMaster credits and certificates to get a full master's degree.

In five to ten years, you will be able to do a whole bunch of additional things including synthesizing your own education for whichever focus you pick. For example, you will be able to stack MicroMasters from several universities in multiple disciplines and synthesize an entire hybrid master's degree. In the same timeframe, you will be able to do the same thing at the bachelor's level.

Whether at the master's or bachelor's level, you can stack the credentials towards the degree or any other objective that you want. In the future, learners will be able to "mix and match" with programs from multiple universities synthesizing their own degree.

But the credential and degree is not the only thing that will become modular. We will also unbundle the clock, admissions, the content, and the costs.

- Clock, because with multiple pathways available for the learner, options for flexible participation, other than the traditional, four-year approach, will abound. Students might complete freshman year online over a period of two years using approaches like Global Freshman Academy, become better prepared for college, and then go to campus for the next three years.

- The admissions and screening process, because if the student can show that she or he has already done the work successfully, for example in a Micro-Master program, which signals capacity to do further work successfully.
- The content. Why does content have to all come from one place? Can you blend course sequences from different providers? Of course you can.
- Costs, because the learner has choice and can use the resources she or he needs in an a la carte fashion.

And universities will also be able to provide more flexibility in the clock, content and access at the bachelor's level. For example, you can have a program for first year college work such as Global Freshman Academy offered by edX and Arizona State University. If you want the option of credit, you pay $50 per course. Then if you pass you can pay $600 per course to get fully transcripted credit for a freshman year. In this process, you have unbundled the clock and content at the undergraduate level. Then, after Global Freshman Academy, you would go off to a second year at Arizona State or other institutions who accept their credit.

Things like this will happen all over the place. Because, when costs go down and quality and personalization go up, you have a powerful new combination of incentives."

► *Mark Milliron*, Civitas

"There are two areas where I think the ecosystem for digitally supported learning will be substantially changed in the next few years.

First, students will be able to access their own analytics. Right now the student's pathway is largely supported internally by colleges, like a 'Degree Map' where the learner gets help along the way, optimizing her learning while she is enrolled. Learners get scaffolding, a way to proceed up and through a program. They can also jump to other programs if their objectives change. And they can then check with Burning Glass to see what the mapping of the new program choice to existing jobs looks like. This will continue to improve. But the essential model is the way we do it today.

The next generation, when we get a large enough data set, an unaffiliated student will be able to tap in and ask, 'Where can I go? Show me other students' pathways and opportunities.' And unaffiliated learners will be able to ask and track these questions and their answers locally, regionally and nationally as well as in groups. The change will be dramatic because it represents a dramatic power shift from institutional to personal control.

Second, there is going to be a lot more of edu-sourcing where learners are helping each other. A company, NearPeer, 'Take Control of Your Learning Today,' is in its early stages. (www.nearpeer.org) It supports a network for students who can find someone who is roughly at their level of knowledge and development. They can then develop peer mentors. But they also can get matched with someone who is 'ahead' of them. And that lets them understand future demands and consequences. Ultimately, learners will be able to 'reach back' and mentor others who are following them.

What we will see is an explosion of learner-driven and learner-centered activity that is supported by data, allowing any user to choose the relationship he prefers with given institutions and services." (www.civitas.com)

▶ *Troy Markowitz*, Portfolium

Troy Markowitz, on the other hand, started working "on the inside" with existing colleges to vastly improve the connections between their "taught" curriculum and learner readiness to work after graduation. He sees tremendous room for further growth and development of their services in the days ahead.

"We are working in an environment of dynamic change for higher education. On the one hand, the traditional model is under increasing pressure when you consider the cost, price, and structure of traditional services. And, in addition to that, the value of the traditional degree as good preparation for work is being seriously questioned. Big companies like Google are removing degree requirements as a precondition for hiring. And Goldman-Sachs has stopped on-campus recruiting. So there is growing pressure on colleges and universities to link their certificates and degrees to career readiness.

There are still career fairs, recruiting boards, and all that kind of thing, but companies and colleges all need to innovate in this space. Because the reality is that students don't have good career information, pathing guidance, and connections to real jobs. For instance, in the natural order of things, who would know that Goldman-Sachs hires engineers.

On the other hand, new third party groups like Portfolium are offering services that bridge the gap between learning and work without vocationalizing higher education. Colleges are sitting on a lot of student performance data relating to job and career readiness that is currently ignored and underutilized. And employers have been contributing to the same problem by not being sufficiently specific in their stated requirements for jobs.

From the campus perspective, the silos of excellence have to be deconstructed and connected to each other to better serve students. For example, progressive universities are not just tracking courses. They are also tracking, validating, and documenting the skills that students are acquiring in class that have historically been ignored, such as critical thinking, teamwork, and problem solving.

We are coming to understand that these "softer" skills may be even more pertinent to job readiness than those recorded on a traditional transcript. Interestingly, as one by-product of these developments, career services are increasingly being tied to alumni affairs and advancement, because that's where the lifelong relationship with the graduate resides.

On the other side of the coin, employers and their understanding of employability has been a problem as well. Jobs have not been analyzed closely for the learning outcomes and capabilities that graduates bring with them. Granular student outcomes have not been tracked and tied to particular jobs.

Portfolium is a bridge between these two, previously disconnected fields. We are connecting with all parties digitally and then leveraging tools that are tangible and useful to learners. And remember, these people are increasingly digital in everything they do. This means it's right up their alley in terms of accessibility.

The bottom line is that any student, traditional or nontraditional, can sign up for free through their college (we are currently working with over 1000 colleges) or independently and immediately create a three-dimensional partnership that links their knowledge and experience with a fuller understanding of the college curriculum and a tighter connection with specific and detailed job requirements. It will also identify gaps in their skills and knowledge to assist in filling those gaps. By the way, this is a free service for the user. But if colleges and employers want access to the data, they have to pay.

An increasing number of employers (we have over 80,000 partners right now) are paying to do competency-based hiring (CBH) through Portfolium. They are looking for the right skill, behavior, and ability 'match,' and the resume doesn't give that picture accurately. Since the data points on a person's portfolio are indexed, that allows the employer to search your data base for the exact match to their jobs using data analytics.

To put it another way, employers are moving from focusing on GPA and class performance to the actual capacity that a person has developed and validated. This is a move away from "take my word for it" and personal connections to evidence-based hiring because a work sample and/or granular data are better indicators than a resume or transcript regarding an individual's work readiness for a given job. This is a shift to valuing 'potential over pedigree.'

Where is it all going? People are asking, "What courses do I need to get the job that I want?' We will increasingly know more and more about what learners want and when they want it. So the ball is moving in that direction. Student debt alone will drive a new order in postsecondary education. People want guaranteed value for their money. And it's beginning to happen.

Colleges need to evolve with the demand, just as special effects people in the movie industry did when they adapted to CGI. Although the faculty is not responsible for getting students jobs, they do have control over the content and underlying skills and behaviors that students are expected to know. Portfolium will help colleges know more about what students know and don't know and help them validate the knowledge and fill the gaps."

▶ *Matt Sigelman*, Burning Glass Technologies

Burning Glass is a deep and ever-expanding source of data about job skills. Founder Matt Sigelman sees this data as central to future program and model developments in the higher education and work force preparation world. And he sees Burning Glass as both a partner with other entities and a sole practitioner in other circumstances as well.

"When you begin to think of higher education as a huge universe of content from multiple sources, everything changes.

The value frame is pulled inside out through a new understanding of the degree and other credentials which are now available on demand. When you think in these terms, the market for higher education broadens markedly as it begins to include not only different demographics but also different patterns of participation. The existing relationship between traditional higher education and the job market has historically been a one-time affair, beginning and ending after you have completed college. But what we see now, with this new universe of content is a lifelong model, a far wider proposition than the traditional model allowed.

Also, there is another kind of diversification going on that further supplements the "broadening" proposition that I just described. Skill sets are becoming hybridized. Skills that traditionally had no business in an occupation, are now showing up. For example, a marketing manager who can build a data base using SEQUEL skills would be very valuable today, where ten years ago that would have been a nonstarter.

All this raises several realities and questions, including:

- What is the 'shape' of an education going forward?
- Are there foundational skills and abilities that equip the learner intellectually to learn throughout life?
- If so, what are they? A hybrid job market will require this.
- Is it the core of the liberal arts that is important?
- Or is it teaching critical thinking and writing that is important?
- Or, is it a question of how the liberal arts are actually experienced so that these cross-cutting intellectual skills are developed consciously as part of a project-based curriculum?

- Will there be a 'funnel' design with the 'foundational skills' up front and specific skill development coming at the end?"

And what could be a more-fitting concluding observation for section three, where we have explored the early stages of a GPS for Learning and Work, than Sigelman's final observation.

"Here's what I know for sure. Being able to adapt on the run is going to be increasingly important downstream for both education and business if they are going to keep up with the learners of the future."

AFTERWORD

L ET ME END BY RETURNING to the beginning. Trying to understand the changes that are discussed in this book and the forces that are driving them is a little bit like skiing in a blizzard with no goggles. Whether you are a policy-maker, an elected official, an educator, a business person, or a "free-range learner," understanding and anticipating this emerging revolutionary world can be as baffling and indecipherable as it is frustrating.

The stakes are high for all of us. On a personal level, however, the stakes for the learner are the highest of all because figuring out your path in this world and then using the right resources to pursue your goals and the future you hope for is based on making the decisions that work best for you. It is the key to a happier and more productive life civically, socially, economically, and personally.

And, although you are indeed skiing in a blizzard of change, *Free-Range Learning* provides goggles to clear some perspective on very basic values and advice along with information about proven resources and services that will stand the test of time. Additionally, the stories shared by the learners, people like you, illuminate the human dimension as well as the practical value of the path forward.

For learners, I advise the following.

- Embrace, value, and take control of your personal learning. (chapter one)
- Learn how to recognize turning points in your life as opportunities to change and grow. (chapter two)
- Find "adult-friendly" colleges, employers, programs which recognize your hidden credentials for the academic and economic value they represent. chapters three, four, and six)
- Use the new employment analytics available to you to get better information about and alignment with the jobs that are available. (chapters seven and eight)
- Resist learning discrimination whenever and wherever you find it. Understand what you have a right to expect from colleges and employers. (chapters five and nine)
- Put yourself in the driver's seat and don't give away the keys to the car!

For policy-makers and elected officials at the federal, state, and local level, this is a time to be thoughtful and deliberate in your response to the tides of change that are sweeping around us. As several of the presidents and entrepreneurs whom I interviewed thoughtfully and accurately observed, the traditional economic and academic model is under severe stress and cannot be sustained in its current state. In the revolutionary "free-range world," the costs of resources and services are decreasing dramatically while their quality is soaring.

The collision of these two realities is leading to new models, new solutions, new relationships, and new understandings that, collectively, add up to a radical re-thinking of just what quality learning is, how we do it, how we recognize it, and how we support readiness to work throughout life. You have seen the early stages of this disruptive process in the pages of this book. And, now that you have read it, you will see examples of the disruption and new services all around you. They need to be carefully considered and fully understood, not rejected out-of-hand because they do not fit the policy or regulatory frameworks of the past.

As one example, consider what I have written and blogged about as "the networked college." (www.rethinkinghighereducation.net). Networking is already happening. Its essence is that the traditional vertical stack of services offered by an institution is no longer sustainable. Few, if any, colleges and universities or employers have the resources to create, maintain, and renew all services to their students, employees and/or customers. The pace of change in technologies and applications is accelerating, driven by forces that originate beyond the boundaries or control of the campus. This creates an environment where the institution must decide what it will be known for, where its quality will lie, and, correspondingly, where it will contract with others for essential services, whether they are Learning Management Systems, Online Program Management Systems, or other services.

In networked arrangements, although the services will appear to be seamless to the learner/user, they will actually be networked behind the scenes through multiple partnerships. Thus the "DNA" of a college will not be wholly owned and operated by that institution. Rather, it will be comprised of multiple strands of services that are wrapped together into a coherent package that is both up-to-date and user-friendly. People who are evaluating institutional quality and/or eligibility will have to accommodate these types and changes, relying on the overall quality and "output" of an institution instead of basing decisions on the quality of the inputs controlled and provided by that institution.

Put another way, the "free-range" experience will be fundamentally different from the traditional campus experience. And in that regard, campuses and these new programs and services will not be comparable and should not be compared on the basis of their "differentness."

Again, it is the results of the educational experience that will, increasingly, be the focus of quality assurance. In this picture, it seems to me that the assessment and validation of learning, wherever and whenever it occurred, is coming to lie at the heart of the sponsored learning experience in the Digital Age. As discussed earlier, excellent assessment will be evidence-based and the result of a reflective process through which the learner and the sponsoring institution assign value to the learning which has been accomplished.

And location will matter less and less. We know that the supply of eighteen year olds will continue to dwindle. (Remember, the high school graduating class of 2036 has already been born.) And adult learners already have a campus. It is their home, their community life, and their workplace. And the free-range world allows them to consciously and deliberately infuse the patterns of their every-day life with learning and related activities that change the arc of their lives. The campus as a substitute community is no longer essential for many people. So, while education will continue to be a social experience as well as a learning experience, where and how that happens will diversify tremendously.

Most colleges that operate through a campus-oriented model face another type of challenge. They must find ways to harness the value of these new services, ways to adapt to the new ecosystem, while being true to their history and mission. This is not easy. But, ultimately, it is essential for survival.

Those of us trying to understand this emerging world, this new ecosystem growing around us and our traditional institutions, know that it is fundamentally different in form and function. As such, it is not to be, and should never be, treated as if it were "the same as" the institutions it is leaving behind. The models must be judged in the future for their "effectiveness," the results they produce, not their inputs, the environment, or the academic model that they offer.

On the one hand, these disruptive forces can make traditional colleges and universities better than ever if they can understand their value and adapt accordingly. On the other hand, the new models allowed and sustained by these disruptive forces will look different. And the challenge they will face is the absolute need to validate their claims of learning and work readiness in ways that gain the confidence of and satisfy educators, employers, learners, and the oversight bodies that evolve to evaluate them. Evidence-based validation of results will become the coin of the realm in the "free-range learning" world.

For employers, educators, and entrepreneurs who want to work in this exciting space, there are significant responsibilities as well. Whether you are public or private, for-profit or nonprofit, you have a deep responsibility to your learners, your employees, and your users. There is a public trust involved, a public trust which must be honored. Lifelong learning is not an off-the-shelf activity. It is about the development of the human potential in each of us. And through all the snowflakes that this blizzard of change throws at us, we must keep our eyes on the promises we make and assure that, wherever possible, the people who entrust their lives and futures to our endeavors get the learning they need and the results that we have promised.

In this time of extraordinary, indeed revolutionary, change comes new experience which will include both great success and error. With experience and mistakes, however, if we learn from them, comes improvement and excellence.

NOTES

1. Peter Smith, *The Quiet Crisis* (San Francisco: Jossey-Bass, 2004).

2. Allen Tough, *The Adult's Learning Projects* (Toronto: The Ontario Institute for Studies in Education, 1969).

3. Peter Smith, *Your Hidden Credentials: The Value of Learning Outside of College* (Washington, DC: Acropolis Books, 1986).

4. Peter Smith, *Your Hidden Credentials*.

5. Peter Smith, *Your Hidden Credentials*.

6. From the 1939 film script of the *The Wizard of Oz* written by Noel Langley, Florence Ryerson, and Edgar Allan Woolf.

7. Peter Smith, *Harnessing America's Wasted Talent* (San Francisco: Jossey-Bass, 2010) p. 95.

8. Peter Smith, *Harnessing America's Wasted Talent*, p. 3.

9. Peter Smith, *Harnessing America's Wasted Talent*.

10. Peter Smith, *Harnessing America's Wasted Talent*

11. Peter Smith, *Your Hidden Credentials*.

12. Peter Smith, *Your Hidden Credentials*, pp.16-17.

13. Peter Smith, *Your Hidden Credentials*.

14. Anya Kamenetz, *The Edupunks' Guide To a DIY Credential*. (http://www.diyubook.com), 2011.

APPENDIX A
URLs Listed by Chapter

CHAPTER ONE
Hiding in Plain Sight

Gallup StrengthsFinder (www.gallupstrengthscenter.com)

CHAPTER THREE
The College Gap

Peter Smith's blogsite (www.rethinkinghighereducation.net)

CHAPTER FIVE
Adult-Friendly Presidents Speak: What You Deserve

Udemy (www.udemy.com)
Charter Oak State College (www.charteroak.edu)
Community College of Vermont (www.ccv.edu)
University of Maryland University College (www.umuc.edu)
Rio Salado College (www.riosalado.edu)
Southern New Hampshire University (www.snhu.edu)

CHAPTER SIX
Getting to the Right College or Credential

Kaplan Calculator (www.portfolio.kaplan.edu/calculator
CAEL PLA Accelerator (www.cael.org/higher-education/
pla-accelerator)

CAEL LearningCounts (www.learningcounts.org)

CAEL Member Institutions (www.cael.org/about-us/membership/cael-members)

The College Navigator (www.nces.ed.gov/collegenavigator/)

The American Council of Education Assessment of Corporate and Militarwww.acenet.edu/news-room/pages/military-Guide-Online.aspx); (https://www2.acenet.edu/credit/)

National College Credit Recommendation Service—State University of New York (www.nationalccrs.org/)

Edupunks Guide to a DIY Credential (https://www.diyubook.com)

StraighterLine (www.straighterLine.com)

College Level Exam Program (www.clep.collegeboard.org)

McGraw-Hill Assessment and Learning Program (www.ALEKS.com)

edX (www.edx.org)

The Open Education Consortium (www.oeconsortium.org)

Saylor Academy (www.sayloracademy.org)

Vermont College of Fine Arts (www.vcfa.edu)

Association of Experiential Education Resources

APEX Adventures (www.apexadventures.com)

(www.LearnThroughExperience.org)

Entrade (www.evoketherapy.com)

Kaleidoscope Learning Circle (www.myklc.com)

National Outdoor Leadership School (www.nols.edu)

Outward Bound (www.outwardbound.org)

Pacific Quest (www.pacificquest.org)

RipplEffect (www.rippleffect.net)

SacredPlay (www.sacredplay.us)

SoundExperience (www.soundexp.org)

Tragedy Assistance Program for Survivors (www.taps.org)

ULead (www.uleadinc.org)

Wolf Connection (www.wolfconnection.org)

World Learning (www.worldlearning.org)

SOME OTHER REFERENCE WEBSITES:

www.aee.org
www.LearnThroughExperience.org
www.OutdoorEd.com
www.aore.org
www.etdalliance.com

CHAPTER SEVEN
Getting the Skills You Need

Burning Glass (www.burningglass.com/research/hybrid-jobs)
General Assembly (www.generalassemb.ly/browse/courses-and-classes)
SwitchUp (www.switchup.org)
Innovate+Educate (www.innovate-educate.org)
Degreed (www.degreed.com)
Credly (www.credly.com)

CHAPTER EIGHT
New Tools for the World of Learning and Work

HelioCampus (www.HelioCampus.com)
Portfolium (www.portfolium.com)
COOL Army (www.cool.army.mil)
COOL Navy (www.cool.navy.mil)
Civilians (www.cool.navy.mil/dciv/index.htm)
Marines (www.cool.navy.mil/usmc)
COOl Air Force (www.afvec.langley.af.mil/afvec/Public/COOL/Default.aspx)
Gallup StrengthsFinder (www.gallupstrengthscenter.com)
Burning Glass (www.burningglass.com)
Full Measure Ed (www.fullmeasureed.com)

CHAPTER 9
The Innovators Speak:
Visions of a New World of Learning and Work

Civitas (www.civitas.com)
NearPeer (www.nearpeer.org)

OTHER URLS

Common Currency (www.commoncurrency.org)
Credential Transparency Initiative (www.
    credentialtransparencyinitiative.org)
Thomas Edison State University (www.tesu.edu)
Excelsior College (www.excelsior.edu/creditbyexam)
Bellevue University (www.bellevue.edu)
SUNY Empire State (www.SUNYEmpireStateCollege.edu)
Parchment (www.parchment.com)

APPENDIX B
Interviews

Interviews done initially for *Your Hidden Credentials*, parts of which have been partially incorporated in *Free-Range Learning*.

Connie Yu Naylor
Elaine McDermott
Nancy Burns
Peg Moore
Phil Barrett

Interviews done in the research for *Free-Range Learning*.

LEARNERS AND USERS
Carol Harrison
Kelley Lawrence
Aaron Roberts
Jennifer Carr
Holly Palmer
Linda West
Irving Gomez
Marianne Shaughnessy
Andrew Hogan
Jason DeForge
Marie Padilla
Keith Waterhouse
Christy Leung

Jearold Hersey
Darren Bradley
Trisha Ward
Alex Olmstead
Maisol Moran
Jason Ransom
Sheila Ann Jordon
Kevin Linn
Danaka Porter
Gabriel Alba

PRESIDENTS
Paul LeBlanc
Ed Klonoski
Joyce Judy
Chris Bustamante
Javier Miyares

ENTREPRENEURS AND INSTITUTIONAL USERS
Brandon Busteed
Matt Sigelman
Chuck Brodsky
Burck Smith
Jonathan Finkelstein
Anant Agarwal
Mark Milliron
Troy Markowitz
Steve Yadzinski
Jeff Burkhart
Kelly Palmer
Beth Doyle
Pat Leonard
Ashley Lyublinski
Brenda Perea

Mary Lou Forward
Devon Ritter
Barbara Lomonaco
Jes Bengtsen
Juli Weber
Lisa Lutz

INDEX

ABOUT THE AUTHOR

PETER SMITH has successfully fought for the recognition and rights of adult learners throughout his career. His record as an innovator in the higher education/lifelong learning space is unparalleled. After a transformational experience as a young man at the Colorado Outward Bound and National Outdoor Leadership Schools, Peter set out on a career path that has put the individual's lived experience at the heart of every learning program he designed for over forty-five years.

Peter designed, launched, and successfully secured state funding for the Community College of Vermont (CCV) in 1970, at the age of twenty-four. The college was designed around the needs of rural adults who had neither the time nor the money to attend college. Operating initially out of churches, high schools, and business locations, the college promoted the assessment of prior experiential learning for academic credit and advanced standing towards the degree. A radical concept at the time, this practice is now well-established and proven. In fact, the record shows that adults who assess their prior learning continue and complete their college degree at significantly higher rates than those who do not. The Community College of Vermont also drew on the surrounding community for faculty members and had access to state and local libraries in an outcomes-based program structure that stood virtually alone in American higher education at the time.

Today, the Community College of Vermont serves more Vermonters than the rest of the Vermont State Colleges system or the University of Vermont collectively. It acts as the "front door" to both the state college system and the University. Its twelve learning centers also operate as economic development centers, melding state economic development programs and higher education programs in a dynamic relationship with business.

Peter's current position, The Orkand Endowed Chair and Professor of Innovative Practices in Higher Education at the University of Maryland University College (UMUC), is a fitting capstone to a career which has spanned five decades of activity in education and politics at the state, national, and global levels. After ten years holding elective office as Vermont State Senator, Lt. Governor, and U S Congressman, Peter returned to higher education in 1991 more committed than ever to putting the learner at the center of the enterprise and emphasizing the critical importance of integrating the learner's lived experience with her academic program.

As the founding president of California State University, Monterey Bay, in 1995, he worked with the faculty and staff to introduce two semesters of service learning as a graduation requirement in an "outcomes-based" academic program. Every learner had to complete a senior project that employed the knowledge gained in their major in a successful and demonstrable way. Today, thirteen years after Peter's departure, the university is still operating as an example of innovation—emphasizing undergraduate research in the sciences, technology, and other areas. As early as their freshman year, students are experiencing action research in the field.

As Assistant Director-General for Education at UNESCO, Peter went global. He supported the effort to "globalize" open educational resources, making access to high quality content free and simple around the world. For his leadership in this and subsequent "open" efforts, Peter was awarded the "Leadership Award for Open Education Excellence" by the global Open Education Consortium in 2015. And early in 2017 he was elected to their board of directors.

Continuing his tradition of disruptive innovation at Kaplan University, Peter established the first online assessment program for prior experiential learning and enriched the lives of thousands of learners who benefitted from the program.

With his national and global experience that spans over forty-five years, Peter is widely acknowledged as a "one-of-a-kind" leader and innovator in adult and lifelong learning. He has never hesitated to move beyond talk to take action, designing and implementing new program structures based on new assumptions and possibilities regarding learning.

Now, with the emergence of the revolution in education, the traditional assumptions about programs for learning are being significantly disrupted. Historically, educational practices that attempted to bridge the gap between adults' lives, college, and work were marginalized because our society was information-poor and these innovative programs defied the dominant academic traditions. Now, the tables are turned. In our information-rich, digitized society, new technologies and data analytics are defining learning opportunities that were previously unimaginable. *Free-Range Learning in the Digital Age* defines this new learning space and give the reader the awareness, knowledge, and tools to use it.

Peter is the one person who can describe this disruptive space through the eyes that matter most: those of the adult learners who needs to blend their living with learning and work to be successful. Describing the driving value behind his career, Peter says, "Some people are truly privileged. To me, privilege means that you have never lost a fight that you didn't pick. And that is true for me. My career has been, and continues to be, focused on people who are losing fights every day that they never asked for."